EFFECTIVE PHRASES FOR PERFORMANCE APPRAISALS

A GUIDE TO SUCCESSFUL EVALUATIONS

AppraisalPro® Books

Publishing Since 1978

NEAL PUBLICATIONS, INC.
127 West Indiana Avenue
Perrysburg, Ohio 43551-1578 U.S.A.

Publishers of

"The #1 Guide to Performance Appraisals"
Doing it right!

"Key Phrases for Powerful Communications"
A Guide of Over 3,500 Phrases for Business,
Professional & Personal Success.

EFFECTIVE PHRASES FOR
PERFORMANCE APPRAISALS

A Guide To Successful Evaluations

Neal Publications, Inc.
127 West Indiana Avenue - P.O. Box 451
Perrysburg, Ohio 43552-0451 U.S.A.
www.nealpublications.com

Fourteenth Edition
Third Printing 2023

ISBN 978-1-882423-20-0
SAN 240-8198
Library of Congress Control Number: 2006211818

FOREWORD

A major responsibility faced by every person in a managerial or supervisory position is the evaluation of employee performance. Increasingly, performance reviews are also being conducted by peers, subordinates and customers. Many individuals have also found the need to make self-evaluations.

This guide is designed to help the appraiser in selecting phrases and words that accurately describe a broad range of critical rating factors.

The phrases contained in this handbook are extremely positive and reflect superior performance. Negative phrases are not included in order to avoid redundancy. Verbs and other wording can simply be substituted to place emphasis on the need for improvement. For example, "excels in delegating routine tasks to subordinates" can easily be changed to, "You can improve your effectiveness by delegating more routine tasks to subordinates."

In addition, the phrases need to be substantiated with factual documentation at every opportunity. As an example, "demonstrates sound cost effectiveness" may be expanded to "demonstrates sound cost effectiveness as shown by your ability to achieve a 10% reduction in departmental expenses through the first six months compared to last year."

(continued)

The same phrase may be used to describe unsatisfactory performance by stating "Since your departmental expenses are 10% over budget for the first six months compared to last year," you are expected to "demonstrate sound cost effectiveness by meeting your year-end budget."

Over the decades, phrases have been continuously revised and added to evaluate ever changing job responsibilities. For example, new electronic technologies are rapidly changing work environments. This edition includes new headings including artificial intelligence, logistics, globalization and other key areas.

While every effort has been made to avoid duplication, some headings are closely interwoven by their very nature. For example, a person using the "Cost Management" section may also find the "Budgets" and "Expense Control" sections helpful.

The guide has been purchased by over one and one-half million users in over 19 countries including individuals, associations, corporations, consultants, educational institutions, law enforcement agencies, libraries, hospitals, departments of the government and military personnel around the world.

CONTENTS

EFFECTIVE PHRASES

I. EFFECTIVE PHRASES

EFFECTIVE PHRASES

EFFECTIVE PHRASES

ACCURACY

recognizes the importance of accuracy

emphasizes the need for accuracy

gives the highest priority to achieving accuracy

is committed to achieving accuracy

focuses on achieving accuracy

holds people accountable for accuracy

performs with a high degree of accuracy

performs with consistent accuracy

achieves results with accuracy and precision

expects precise results

maintains high statistical accuracy

expects perfection

strives for perfection

excels in achieving perfection

pursues exactness

is committed to flawless execution

avoids mistakes and errors

continuously strives to reduce errors

excels in uncovering errors

is quick to correct mistakes and errors

develops realistic tolerance levels

(continued)

ACCURACY

conforms to strict tolerances

meets precise standards

maintains a very high accuracy standard

meets rigid specifications

keeps accurate records

maintains accurate documentation

provides explicit documentations

is meticulous with detail

gives meticulous attention to detail

excels in detail checking

forecasts with extreme accuracy

uses state-of-the-art methods for accurate forecasting

uses sound statistical methods to forecast with accuracy

excels in accurately forecasting future situations

is very accurate in forecasting future trends

is highly regarded for true and accurate predictions

makes accurate predictions about future trends, directions and developments

ACHIEVEMENT

achieves optimal levels of personal performance and accomplishment

strives for a high achievement level

maintains a record of significant achievement

maintains a record of substantial achievement

is widely recognized for achievements

is a solid achiever

is a high achiever

is achievement-oriented

is achievement-driven

achieves consistent effectiveness

is a consistent achiever

achieves consistently high results

achieves consistent and favorable results

achieves lasting results

excels in achieving outstanding results

achieves bottom-line results

turns opportunities into results

focuses on results

is strategically focused on achieving results

(continued)

ACHIEVEMENT

delivers reliable and sustainable results

delivers results

excels in developing programs that deliver results

demonstrates an ability to achieve desired results

directs efforts to achieve powerful results

attains results without negative side effects

attains results through positive actions

achieves organizational excellence

produces an exceptional level of accomplishments

provides strong evidence of specific accomplishments

possesses a record of significant accomplishments

accomplishes more with fewer people

exceeds the norm

accomplishes consistent and optimal outcomes

provides exceptional outcomes

produces a tangible, positive impact

ADMINISTRATION

demonstrates a high level of administrative competence

is skilled in performing a broad range of administrative duties

provides a wide range of administrative services

demonstrates strong administrative skills

provides outstanding administrative relief to management

is a key member of the administrative staff

achieves high administrative output

is continuously examining administrative effectiveness and seeking better procedures

develops policies and procedures to improve department

establishes and follows clear administrative rules and regulations

keeps policy and procedure manuals current

enumerates and specifies procedures for implementing and administering policies

ensures compliance with all policies and procedures

develops successful administrative strategies

is continuously examining administrative services

(continued)

ADMINISTRATION

encourages administrative efficiency and effectiveness

ensures that administrative work areas are designed for maximum efficiency

is skilled in optimizing systems to gain greater efficiency

excels in simplifying and reducing paperwork

excels in eliminating unnecessary paperwork

is rapidly reducing paperwork

avoids unnecessary correspondence

responds promptly to correspondence

avoids burdening management with administrative details

effectively uses exceptional reporting to keep management informed

supplies necessary support services

is able to provide a broad range of back-up support

ensures that back-up support is available to maintain essential services

maintains a strong system of internal controls

is skilled in handling administrative matters with other departments

keeps other departments fully informed of related activities

ADMINISTRATION

works well with other administrative personnel at national, regional and global locations

is a strong participant in administrative staff meetings

shows initiative in expressing comments at staff meetings

is skilled in applying basic statistical methods

makes effective use of statistical applications

is continuously searching for new equipment to increase work capacity and reduce costs

provides strong information processing capabilities

is very knowledgeable and proficient in using a wide range of software programs

keeps abreast of new techniques to improve administrative efficiency

is eager to use new technology for increased efficiency

excels in increasing the use of sophisticated administrative technologies

utilizes improved technology for administrative support

is continuously improving logistics and information systems

ANALYTICAL SKILLS

demonstrates a strong power of analytical reasoning

displays strong analytical qualities

demonstrates a strong ability to analyze problems

is very methodical in solving problems

utilizes a variety of analytical techniques to solve problems

displays a strong knowledge of statistical techniques in solving problems

excels in mathematical calculations

handles mathematical calculations with speed and accuracy

excels in analyzing and adjusting work procedures for maximum efficiency

analyzes conditions thoroughly and reaches independent decisions

concentrates on analyzing essential facts

excels in tedious research

effectively analyzes relevant information

applies sound analytical thinking

excels in analytical thinking

ARTIFICIAL INTELLIGENCE (AI)

possesses strong technical and analytical skills needed to achieve success in AI

displays a strong knowledge of AI modeling, prediction and decision making potential of AI

is highly skilled in developing data bases for future AI applications

demonstrates strong AI leadership abilities

recognizes the tremendous cost saving benefits of AI

is using AI to achieve cost effective and efficient solutions

is placing a high priority on implementing AI

is skilled in obtaining management approval and funds for transitions to AI

is implementing AI to allow employees to concentrate on high value work

is exploring the applications of AI in virtually every department of our organization

is keeping our organization highly competitive in AI development

is keeping our organization a leader in AI applications

is effectively using AI for maintenance scheduling and to predict warning signs

is implementing AI driven innovation

is making effective use of AI to improve our competitive strengths

(continued)

ARTIFICIAL INTELLIGENCE (AI)

is implementing AI to provide more personalized support to all customers

is demonstrating strong skills as a team member implementing AI

is a major contributor to the AI implementation team

is working closely with department to ensure a smooth transition to AI

maintains an excellent relationship with all AI technical personnel

excels in helping employees overcome misperceptions and concerns about AI

is strong in assisting employees to successfully implement transitions to AI

is demonstrating powerful skills in training employees to accept and administer AI applications

makes powerful presentations at AI training sessions

is making effective use of AI in global operations with different currencies and other variances

is using AI to overcome language barriers in global translations

is using AI to keep all offices, departments, plants and field personnel informed of common interests

is making effective use of AI in voice recognition

ASSIGNMENTS

is very effective in assigning employees, materials and equipment

matches assignments with employees' talents

conveys priority status when assigning duties and projects

recognizes the need to concentrate on high priority assignments

places high priority projects on a special assignment basis

is always reliable in successfully completing all assignments

is exceptionally reliable and trustworthy when given an assignment

demonstrates the ability to successfully complete a wide range of assignments

demonstrates a systematic approach in carrying out assignments

demonstrates accuracy, thoroughness and orderliness in performing work assignments

displays strong initiative in carrying out assignments

volunteers for extra work and demanding assignments

is eager to take on new assignments

is eager to accept challenging assignments

views assignments as an opportunity for growth

BUDGETS

provides valuable input for budgets based on past experience, current situations and future trends

weighs a vast amount of critical information when planning budgets

gives strong budget consideration to the allocation of critical resources

prepares budgets based on available resources and organizational goals

is methodical in preparing a line item budget of controllable expenditures

plans budgets based on realistic projections

establishes realistic budget objectives

is very accurate in forecasting budget requirements

applies sound accounting principles in preparing budgets

is very accurate in planning and controlling budget allocations

demonstrates strong budgeting skills

effectively manages department budget

weighs budget limitations in all decision making

makes operating decisions in conformance with budget limitations

is reliable in consistently meeting budget deadlines

BUDGETS

is skillful in justifying budget requests in detail

deals promptly and effectively with budget variances

is skilled in justifying budget variances

is able to justify budget variances due to uncontrollable circumstances

recognizes that budget requests are subject to unforeseen circumstances

excels in continuously monitoring budget variances

gives close attention to monitoring budget variances and plans appropriate adjustments

takes prompt actions to avoid budget variances

keeps employees aware of the need for budget conformance

is a strong enforcer of budget conformance

holds employees accountable for both planning and use of allocated funds

makes a strong effort to keep expenditures within budget

makes effective use of computer generated budget charts and graphs

is very proficient in making maximum use of information technology in the budget process

COACHING AND COUNSELING

shows sincere interest in employees and the solution to their problems

is highly regarded by employees for sharing concerns, problems and opportunities

is well regarded by employees seeking advice

is frequently sought for opinions

is highly regarded for expert consultation

gives sound, practical advice

is always willing to provide a wealth of solid advice

gives helpful guidance to employees

guides employees to proper resources whenever help is needed

lends support and guidance to employees

inspires voluntary support and guidance to employees

assists employees in career assessment

is a strong proponent of employee coaching and counseling

excels in effective coaching and counseling of employees

displays strong coaching skills

uses sound coaching techniques to solve disciplinary problems

COACHING AND COUNSELING

is very enthusiastic when coaching employees

is an inspiring and influential coach

effectively coaches toward achievement

is very effective in coaching for greater
job success

provides continuous coaching

is highly regarded as a sincere, trusted and
capable mentor

is a strong mentor

displays excellent mentoring skills

is a trusted counselor

is highly trusted as an experienced counselor

demonstrates exceptional skills in
employee counseling

excels in providing wise counsel
and guidance

makes effective use of meetings and seminars
to provide counseling on common employee
issues

effectively uses counseling techniques
and skills

is a respected advisor and counselor

is highly regarded by employees as an
excellent counselor

COMMUNICATION SKILLS

excels in effective and positive communications

communicates openly, forcefully and effectively

communicates clearly and concisely

communicates clearly and forcefully

communicates with strong credibility

communicates with credibility and confidence

communicates with a positive impact

is a competent communicator

demonstrates an ability to perform and communicate

communicates high expectations

effectively communicates expectations

communicates effectively with all levels of management

communicates clear management expectations

effectively communicates management decisions to achieve understanding and acceptance

communicates clear strategic direction

effectively communicates goals and interplay of ideas and concepts

provides an intellectual atmosphere conducive to the stimulation and interchange of ideas

encourages a free exchange of ideas

COMMUNICATION SKILLS

excels in facilitating group discussions

is very convincing in communicating before groups of any size

excels in communicating with individuals and groups

is a skilled meeting participant

demonstrates strong committee procedures and techniques

excels in intercommunications and interactions

makes appropriate use of formal vs. informal communications

maintains an open dialog with employees

ensures that communications are kept open

keeps lines of communications open

values open communications

encourages open communications to achieve mutual understandings

strives for openness

develops and maintains two-way communications

is a skillful interviewer

asks penetrating questions

prevents unproductive responses

(continued)

COMMUNICATION SKILLS

displays effective listening skills

makes effective use of listening skills

is an empathetic listener

avoids communication breakdowns

excels in gaining approvals and authorizations

effectively explains and interprets
organizational policies and procedures

enforces company policies without creating
negative reactions

effectively communicates authority under
difficult circumstances

communicates effectively in high
stress situations

effectively communicates upward,
downward and laterally

communicates effectively both
horizontally and vertically

keeps other departments informed of
developments affecting their functions

excels in relating well to others

excels in interpersonal communications

effectively communicates with co-workers

communicates confidently with superiors,
peers and subordinates

utilizes all channels of communication

COMMUNICATION SKILLS

demonstrates good judgment in selecting the proper mode of communications

makes effective use of the telephone, and electronic mail

knows when to cover topics by letter, e-mail, or phone

demonstrates proper telephone techniques and etiquette

effectively translates complex information into common terms

is able to communicate complex information into user-friendly terms

excels in verbal and nonverbal communications

uses proper oral and written language

possesses a strong vocabulary

possesses strong bilingual skills

is able to communicate in other languages

responds quickly to all oral and written communications

responds quickly to external activities and events

responds promptly to requests

is assertive without being overly aggressive

is able to communicate assertively without causing negative reactions

(continued)

COMMUNICATION SKILLS

makes the best impression in all situations

is a sought after speaker

is widely recognized as an excellent speaker

is an excellent spokesperson for the organization

is a respected representative of the organization

conveys a favorable image of the organization

excels in dealing with the public

effectively represents the organization in community support activities

is highly skilled in expressing the organization's views at industry events

enhances the organization's image by giving exceptional speeches to outside groups

conveys an impression which reflects favorably upon the public relations of the organization

uses communication skills to bolster the organization's image

strives to enhance the organization's reputation

promotes organizational policies, the quality of its products and its reputation

COMPETENCY

demonstrates competent performance

displays distinctive competence

projects a special competence

shows proven competence

focuses on core competencies

enhances core strengths

demonstrates strong interpersonal competence

excels in advancing core strategies

focuses on strengths

effectively capitalizes on strengths

accentuates strengths

maximizes personal strengths

demonstrates a high level of expertise

demonstrates strong personal effectiveness

believes in self

projects self-confidence

is very confident of abilities

displays accurate self-perception of abilities

handles challenging situations with confidence

faces major challenges with confidence

(continued)

COMPETENCY

possesses the capacity to meet major
challenges

uses abilities to the fullest

excels in the effective application of skills

demonstrates highly sophisticated
skills and strategies

possesses specialized skills

displays many solid skills

is highly skilled in all phases of job

excels in operational skills

is especially effective in the development
and use of supportive skills

sharpens and continuously updates skills

is extremely capable

is uniquely qualified

is eminently qualified

builds employee confidence

attends seminars and workshops
to improve personal competence

devotes appropriate time and effort to the
development of professional competence

COMPUTER SKILLS

possesses a strong knowledge of computer fundamentals

is strong in computer fundamentals

possesses extensive computer experience

is strong in computer expertise

is giving a very high priority to computer protection

is taking strong measures to secure computer systems and information

keeps well aware of cyber security threats and protections

excels in converting common tasks to computer processing

is able to skillfully transfer manual functions to computerized systems

is computer literate

takes full advantage of computer programs to maximize productivity

is able to build powerful databases

excels in protecting databases

ensures that computers are used to generate meaningful information and increase efficiency

utilizes the power of computers

understands computer applications

(continued)

COMPUTER SKILLS

works faster and smarter using powerful computer software

makes full use of software capabilities

excels in desktop publishing

makes effective use of desktop computer graphics

excels in creating user-friendly programs

maximizes the benefits of computer techniques

makes effective use of time-saving computer techniques

effectively identifies computer support requirements

ensures that computer back-up systems are fully in use

makes effective use of computer equipment and facilities

provides sound advice when purchasing new computers and equipment

keeps alert to new computer hardware

keeps abreast of new software applications

makes effective use of on-line resources

is skilled in navigating the Internet to provide essential information

understands and effectively utilizes the World Wide Web

COMPUTER SKILLS

is very knowledgeable in the intricacies of the Internet

makes innovative use of the Internet

is highly skilled in navigating the Internet to find relevant information

excels in diagnosing and solving computer malfunctions

demonstrates a strong ability to solve computer problems

displays strong skills in solving hardware and software malfunctions

excels in computer trouble shooting

encourages employee acceptance and use of computers

excels in overcoming resistance to new uses of information technology

is very skilled in providing computer training

excels in computer training for both individuals and groups

ensures the proper training of computer operators

excels in instructing new employees of commonly used computer programs

is a valuable resource for assisting other computer users

excels in assisting others with computer problems

COOPERATION

works well in cooperation with others for the benefit of the organization

encourages cooperative organizational action

encourages organization-wide cooperation

cooperates effectively with other departments

cooperates effectively with multiple superiors

works harmoniously and effectively with staff members

builds strong working relationships

is extremely cooperative with associates

is always willing to provide back-up support

is very cooperative in helping new employees learn and adjust

develops a strong working rapport with others

is always willing to help others

is cooperative and open-minded in working with others

works effectively with others

works in close harmony with others

is able to gain the cooperation of others

is glad to share expertise

shares ideas and techniques

is highly cooperative in sharing information

COOPERATION

inspires cooperation and confidence

cooperates with enthusiasm

displays a harmonious and cooperative spirit

is skillful in bringing uncooperative workers together in a spirit of cooperation

promotes cooperative behavior and team efforts

excels in joint efforts

promotes productive cooperation

is always willing to extend the fullest cooperation

builds cooperation

is cooperative and constructive

competes and cooperates

effectively implements plans with harmony and cooperation

receives and carries out tasks in a cooperative manner

is very cooperative in supporting new policies, plans and procedures

COORDINATION

is demonstrating a strong ability to coordinate with critical departments to ensure a unified approach to achieving common objectives

excels in striving for the synchronization of all departments and organizations efforts

excels in the orderly synchronization of the organization

ensures that all plans are coordinated to make certain that objectives are harmonized

keeps all aspects of the organization in balance

is very successful in synchronizing the efforts of employees

strives for unified efforts

is highly skilled in performing all coordination duties

makes effective use of coordinating skills to simplify efforts and avoid duplications of functions

is very effective in coordinating both horizontally and vertically

ensures that all departments are working in close harmony and effectiveness

is highly effective in the coordination of resources, personnel, equipment and operations

makes effective use of meetings and committees to ensure unified efforts

COORDINATION

maintains excellent communications with key departments

effectively coordinates the scheduling and completion of annual, quarterly and monthly reports

keeps critical departments informed by distributing meeting minutes, bulletins and reports

is effective in developing and distributing a calendar of major activities and deadlines

closely monitors the meetings of critical deadlines

understands the mutual interdependence of departments

is skilled in arranging for the temporary transfer of employees for backup support

thinks in terms of the entire organization

displays a thorough knowledge of the organization

builds a strong climate of coordination

keeps key personnel informed of possible crises that may develop due to shortages, strikes etc.

ensures that manufacturing and marketing are informed of trends such as styles, designs, packaging etc.

ensures that marketers are given advance notice of upcoming programs

(continued)

COORDINATION

keeps financial departments informed of the
need for funds to cover new developments
and programs

ensures that vital internet data bases are
continuously updated for the benefit
of marketers and consumers

keeps management well informed of significant
information

is an excellent source of essential information

keeps managers informed of industry
developments that may affect the organization

keeps key personnel informed of developments
that will affect the organization such as
legislation and environment concerns

is very effective in keeping management
informed of competitive developments

is highly skilled in providing management with
vital information for corporate reports

keeps public relations informed of timely
information for potential release

is very experienced in planning for large
meetings, conferences and conventions

excels in coordinating the presentations of
various departments at conferences

effectively coordinates information to outlying
offices and field personnel

keeps key departments well informed of
feedback from field personnel

COST MANAGEMENT

effectively controls costs through economical utilization of personnel, materials and equipment

is very knowledgeable in knowing the standards, assumptions and measurement methods of generally accepted cost accounting principles

ensures that generally accepted cost accounting principles are followed

displays a good working knowledge of cost accounting fundamentals

is highly competent in developing critical accounting policies

pursues effective cost oversight responsibilities

is highly competent in analyzing cost information

demonstrates sound financial discipline

takes prompt action to meet organizational cost objectives

demonstrates aggressive cost management

ensures that all expenditures are in the best interests of the organization

recognizes the cost implication of all management decisions

demonstrates good judgment in making cost decisions

gives close attention to cost implications of decisions

(continued)

COST MANAGEMENT

excels in determining the cost impact of decisions

excels in providing managers with the cost information needed for decision making

is very proficient in providing essential cost information to various departments

ensures that all managers understand their cost responsibilities

ensures that managers consider cost control as a key responsibility

excels in profit-oriented decisions

is keenly aware of the impact of expenses on profits

is skilled in developing techniques to improve profitability

demonstrates a strong ability to strengthen cost profit ratios

excels in cost-benefit analysis

strives for maximum return on investment

offers continuous and solid suggestions for enhancing profits

makes maximum use of allocated funds

is very effective in closely monitoring overhead costs

gives close attention to both direct and indirect costs

COST MANAGEMENT

monitors both fixed and variable costs continuously

gives close attention to cyclical costs

demonstrates sound cost effectiveness

is very cost conscious

excels in reducing costs

sets realistic cost priorities

is very accurate in estimating costs

is very effective in monitoring cost constraints

deals effectively with fiscal restraints

excels in cost containment

excels in communicating cost improvement programs

gives full support to cost improvement programs

seeks cost improvement measures from employees

is continuously searching for hidden cost improvements

excels in uncovering hidden cost savings

strives for potential cost savings

effectively identifies areas needing cost reductions

is strong in identifying relevant costs

(continued)

COST MANAGEMENT

strives to reduce operating expenses

is very conscious of the need for cost justifications

enforces strict cost justifications

gives sound consideration to costs when procuring materials, supplies and services

maintains close inventory control to reduce costs

effectively commits resources of staff funds and time

achieves cost reductions through improved scheduling of personnel

focuses on continuous cost reductions without sacrificing quality

demonstrates success in reducing costs while maintaining high quality

is very effective in developing internal cost control systems

excels in establishing standardized operating and cost control systems

is strong in developing sound controls for greater cost efficiencies

maintains strong internal cost controls

takes strict measures to ensure effective cost controls

develops strong cost control measures to ensure results

COST MANAGEMENT

excels in identifying and controlling critical cost elements

enforces all internal controls

ensures strict conformance to cost control programs

maintains effective cost control

monitors all controllable costs very closely

excels in waste reduction management

is very effective in controlling waste and spoilage

excels in waste reduction

takes strong measures to eliminate waste

makes strong efforts to eliminate waste

takes strong measures to protect the organization against cost accounting irregularities

excels in developing effective audit controls

is very effective in developing and implementing operational cost audits

implements and closely monitors audit cost controls

adheres to sound ethical and auditing principles

CREATIVITY

demonstrates a high degree of originality and creativity

displays creative imagination

displays active imagination

demonstrates imaginative insight

provides valuable insights

demonstrates creative strength

develops creative and successful strategies

seeks creative alternatives

challenges conventional practices

follows a variety of approaches in activities and techniques

explores new paths, procedures and approaches

develops creative and unique programs

discovers new approaches

applies creative approaches to everyday situations

excels in developing new perspectives

is clever and imaginative when confronted with obstacles

is able to develop creative solutions to challenging problems

develops creative solutions to difficult problems

CREATIVITY

is very inventive

is continuously experimenting

excels in creative experimentation

is very creative in developing unique courses of action

originates and develops constructive ideas

effectively turns ideas into realities

initiates good conceptional ideas with practical applications

excels in developing spontaneous ideas

originates unsought ideas

seeks new ideas and approaches

stimulates ideas

promotes the flow of good ideas

is receptive to new ideas

offers many creative ideas

generates fresh ideas

initiates fresh ideas

excels in nurturing new ideas

displays a sense of inquiry

maintains a high level of curiosity

creates interest

(continued)

CREATIVITY

displays a strong power of observation

is heavily relied upon for creative support

is highly talented in providing creative support

is often asked for creative opinions

provides a broad range of creative services

taps the creative potential of a group

excels in tapping the creative potential
of employees

creates unique value

creates opportunities

creates high expectations

promotes an environment conducive to
creativity

encourages an environment for creative
excellence

promotes a creative climate

builds a department that fosters creativity

is a highly creative member of the department

excels in releasing the creativity of employees

welcomes creative ideas from subordinates

CUSTOMER SERVICE

recognizes customer service as a critical factor in marketing success

gives customer service a high priority

recognizes the vital role of customer service

recognizes the value of extraordinary customer service

uses customer service to gain a competitive edge

provides exceptional customer service

provides the highest level of customer service

provides premium customer service

impresses customers with excellent service

demonstrates strong customer service skills

makes customers feel satisfied and appreciated

ensures that customers are completely satisfied

delivers consistent and value-added services to customers

keeps customers fully informed of any factors affecting a scheduled delivery

resolves customer problems at early stages

excels in solving customer problems

(continued)

CUSTOMER SERVICE

handles customer complaints promptly and effectively

provides quick responses to customer complaints

handles customer complaints with tact and diplomacy

uses strong listening skills when handling customer complaints

maintains a positive approach in handling customer problems

remains calm and professional when dealing with difficult customer situations

is able to regain customer loyalty under difficult circumstances

uses complaints to provide valuable customer feedback

effectively handles unreasonable requests and demands from customers

is skilled in refusing customer requests while presenting alternative solutions

excels in handling customer inquires

provides responsive follow-up service

is able to solve problems without having customers contact management uses the most penetrating and objective evaluations to arrive at sound decisions

makes sound decisions when faced with multi-faceted problems

effectively weighs risks, uncertainties and assumptions

assembles all available facts before making decisions

takes decisive action based on well documented facts

seeks staff input for decision making

makes decisions with confidence

communicates decisions with confidence

displays firmness in making decisions

makes decisions with strong convictions

supports convictions with sufficient force

is reliable in making sound decisions

makes sound decisions under pressure

makes inventive and resourceful decisions

develops resourceful decisions

excels in making resource-allocated decisions

is willing to make difficult and unpopular decisions

(continued)

DECISION MAKING

is able to effectively communicate unpopular decisions

demonstrates an ability to effectively influence key decision makers

is very skilled in obtaining support for decisions

avoids hasty decisions

makes sound decisions in the absence of detailed instructions

weighs alternative decisions before taking action

weighs alternative decisions before making commitments

gives careful consideration to tactical alternatives

considers flexible alternatives

weighs numerous scenarios before making decisions

makes decisions based on sound logic

is able to effectively weigh theoretical versus practical considerations and applications

effectively uses computer simulation to assist in decision making

excels in considering diversified approaches before taking action

follows disciplined approaches

is very successful in making intuitive decisions

DECISION MAKING

weighs the possibility of unintended consequences

foresees the consequences of decisions

recognizes potential adverse consequences of decisions

recognizes the financial impact of decisions

excels in foreseeing the effects of decisions

weighs strategic ramifications of decisions

is very skilled in formulating solutions to difficult issues

concentrates on developing solutions

excels in seeking solutions

develops fresh solutions

excels in suggesting optional solutions

exercises a wide range of decision making control

is very decisive

strives to improve decisiveness

ensures conformance to all decisions

encourages decision making at lowest possible level

DELEGATING

delegates to improve organizational effectiveness

delegates to maximize organizational strengths

delegates to build a strong and self-functioning department

recognizes the importance of working through subordinates

encourages delegation

demonstrates effective delegation techniques

is a strong delegator

gives subordinates the authority needed to effectively carry out delegated responsibilities

empowers employees with the authority and resources to achieve results

provides subordinates with the resources needed to accomplish results

excels in empowering team members with responsibility and authority

delegates with clearly defined responsibility and authority

effectively delegates responsibility

delegates while maintaining control

delegates without micromanaging

prevents reverse delegation

encourages subordinates to solve their own problems

knows when and what to delegate

makes effective use of delegation during vacation periods

delegates routine tasks to subordinates

makes effective use of secretarial support

delegates to match personal strengths

matches assignments with employee skills

delegates to the proper person

effectively delegates unpleasant tasks

delegates to evaluate employee potential

effectively assesses delegation capability

delegates to improve job satisfaction of subordinates

delegates to keep jobs interesting and challenging

delegates to motivate

delegates to build subordinates

helps subordinates gain visibility

creates a high degree of trust with subordinates

DEPENDABILITY

is consistent, dependable and accurate in carrying out responsibilities to a successful conclusion

displays industriousness, conscientiousness and dependability in performing tasks

is reliable in meeting schedules and deadlines

accepts all responsibilities fully and meets deadlines

completes all projects and reports on time

is consistently punctual

is regular in attendance

is always fully prepared

meets responsibilities promptly

achieves results when confronted with major responsibilities and limited resources

utilizes all available resources to achieve results

is reliable in achieving results during emergency situations

is dependable in using proven methods and techniques to achieve results

is very dependable in accomplishing results during the absence of superiors

is extremely valuable in providing back-up support during vacation periods and absences

DEPENDABILITY

is reliable in accomplishing the best
possible results

attains results regardless of the task levels

is able to achieve results despite obstacles

generates greater success in highly complex
situations

displays rigid self-discipline

makes verbal commitments that are consistent
with actions

fulfills all commitments

meets expectations

is very dependable and conscientious

is a strong and reliable member of
the department

is extremely reliable and supportive

is always trusted to provide support

is very trustworthy

is always reliable in doing the job and
any other special tasks

is reliable in successfully completing
all projects

effectively follows-up on given tasks

is exceptionally reliable and trustworthy when
given a project

DEVELOPMENT

excels in selecting and developing individuals with high potential talent

excels in recognizing employees with strong growth potential

is fast developing a department known for its credibility and employee skills

identifies staff development needs

recognizes development levels and ability of staff and others

encourages broad development of employees

encourages individual growth and development of employees

excels in orienting new employees

initiates and establishes personal growth and career paths

excels in developing career paths

plans for effective career development

deals effectively with different career stages of employees

plans for future development and accomplishment

focuses on future development

provides many opportunities for development

shows a strong interest in professional development

DEVELOPMENT

is eager to participate in professional development programs

is a strong participant in continuing education programs

seeks personal growth and development

is ideally positioned for personal growth

strives for continuous self-development

understands personal strengths and weaknesses

excels in identifying individual strengths

excels in developing hidden strengths of employees

reinforces employee strengths

cultivates strengths of subordinates

displays an ability to turn weaknesses into strengths

concentrates development on weak areas

makes strong efforts to bring out the best in every employee

makes effective use of lateral transfers to offer fresh challenges

uses job rotation to effectively develop employees

shows genuine interest in employee progress

effectively tracks employee progress

(continued)

DEVELOPMENT

excels in developing mutual development expectations

fosters a climate of continuous improvement

strives to continuously upgrade talents

is strong in cultivating talent

develops talented and committed employees

is skilled in developing existing talent

exploits under-utilized capabilities

maximizes employees' energy and capabilities

encourages managers to develop subordinates

develops subordinates into high achievers

effectively recommends methods to assist subordinates in overcoming weaknesses

builds successful subordinates

makes winners out of subordinates

inspires subordinates to achieve their fullest potential

assists subordinates in reaching new levels of skills, knowledge and attitudes

assists subordinates in applying new skills, techniques and understandings

assesses the continuous development and effectiveness of subordinates

develops managerial candidates

produces many managers

gives proper attention to personnel succession planning

develops qualified successors

makes accurate assessments of training needs

encourages enthusiasm in the training of personnel

uses a wide variety of training methods

develops innovative and powerful training techniques

is very proficient in both on-the-job and classroom training

encourages employees to improve abilities for greater responsibility

encourages employees to strive for continuous improvement

encourages employees to become promotable

enhances employee prospects for advancement

effectively uses job rotation to develop employees for greater responsibility

encourages employees to acquire proper skills, attitudes and knowledge

builds on the positive

ENVIRONMENTAL

displays a strong awareness of environmental concerns

ensures that all actions are safe and environmentally responsible

takes strong measures to minimize environment impacts

strives to continuously reduce the environmental impact of operations

is committed to environmentally sound practices

keeps abreast of all environmental concerns

is environmentally conscious

keeps informed of current government compliance issues

practices great vigilance in conforming to all laws and regulations

enforces all government environmental regulations

adheres closely to all environmental policies concerning discharges, emissions and exposure

takes proper measures to avoid spills and releases

is careful to follow proper storage procedures

is skilled in training employees for environmental emergencies adheres to ethical principles that reflect the highest standards of organizational and individual behavior

displays a strong commitment to the organization's mission and values

keeps in strict conformance to the organization's values statement

ensures compliance with the organization's values statement

effectively communicates the organization's culture, values and beliefs

promotes a rigorous ethics culture

builds a value-driven culture

encourages long-term value creation

promotes shared values

assigns a top priority to ethics

promotes high standards for honesty, integrity and fairness

is committed to honesty and integrity

hires employees of high integrity

displays an unwavering commitment to high ethical standards

is committed to ensuring the highest ethical standards

displays a dedication to the highest standards of ethical behavior

(continued)

ETHICS

displays high values and ethics

maintains the highest standards of ethics

takes responsible actions based on high ethics

is regarded as highly trustful, sincere and honest

maintains high personal integrity

demonstrates integrity

maintains high credibility

maintains a high degree of ethical conduct

builds a high degree of ethical trust

is committed to a high standard of professional ethics

creates an ethical work environment

keeps alert to any conflicts of interest

is a strong contributor to good business conduct

follows high standards of ethical behavior in all company relationships

communicates ethical values both inside and outside the organization

maintains high standards of integrity with customers, suppliers and employees

EVALUATION SKILLS

establishes clear and meaningful criteria or standards for effective performance

establishes clear performance objectives and evaluation criteria

develops clear performance criteria

develops key performance factors for fair comparisons

establishes credible standards

excels in creating specific performance measures

establishes credible measurement methods

uses sophisticated methods to measure productivity

monitors performance accurately against objectives

effectively makes quantitative determinations of skills

gives proper attention to evaluating both new and long-term employees

maintains an accurate knowledge of worker's skills

recognizes high potential employees

assesses accurate potential

identifies individuals who have a capacity to perform

(continued)

EVALUATION SKILLS

recognizes special talents and capabilities of employees

effectively identifies goal achievers

understands accomplishments, strengths and weaknesses of employees

provides management with accurate information concerning the strengths and weaknesses of employees

effectively assesses employee resources, strengths and competencies

identifies and discusses weaknesses of staff members

assesses employee growth on a regular basis

evaluates throughout the year with open employee communications

gives continuous follow-up to appraisal concerns

effectively tracks performance

evaluates accurate employee effectiveness

produces highly accurate assessments

is careful not to focus on the appraisal system instead of improving employee performance

rates on the basis of performance and not personality

effectively rates job performance and not the individual

EVALUATION SKILLS

limits all evaluations carefully to on-the-job performance

shows significant frequency differences in appraising employees

avoids deceptively inflated reviews

distinguishes between ability and actual performance

effectively documents observations with specific examples

recognizes the need for accurate documentation in the evaluation process

documents performance with skill

ensures that all criticism is fully documented

effectively evaluates others without creating resentment or negative responses

gives recognition to deserving individuals and is quick to recognize extra effort

effectively grants rewards on the basis of objective accomplishment

identifies clearly the main attributes of strong performers

directs performance appraisals toward the self-improvement of employee

encourages and facilitates self-evaluation

prepares highly accurate self-evaluations

effectively critiques own work

(continued)

EVALUATION SKILLS

makes effective use of performance
evaluations to inspire greater achievement

effectively uses performance reviews as
a motivational tool

plans for appraisal interview

gives proper attention to performance
appraisal interviews

anticipates employee reactions to appraisal
interview

prepares for possible negative reaction to
evaluation review

excels in establishing feedback systems for
evaluation results

measures and assesses accurate employee
feedback

identifies individuals needing periodic retraining

excels in providing evaluation training

ensures that all evaluators are properly trained

ensures the proper storage and retrieval of
appraisal records

recognizes the legal implications of
performance appraisals

ensures that all evaluators recognize
the importance of performance appraisals

EXPENSE CONTROL

is consistently able to keep variable expenses within budget

excels in monitoring and controlling expenses

is able to control expenses without lowering accomplishments

is skilled in revising expense policies to reflect increasing costs

ensures that all appropriate employees clearly understand current expense policies

shows good judgment in allowing excessive expenses due to uncontrollable circumstances

is very successful in obtaining approval for unusually high but justified expenses

makes a strong effort to avoid unnecessary or excessive expenses

strives to improve operating expenses

is skilled in uncovering hidden expenses

excels in closely tracking expenses

plans travel, entertainment and related expenses to achieve maximum cost effectiveness

submits all expense reports on time

is very reliable and accurate in providing supporting expense receipts

is reliable in closely following expense policies

FEEDBACK

seeks feedback from all levels of the organization

promotes feedback among employees, customers and clients

is a strong believer in the value of feedback

takes feedback very seriously

seeks employees feedback following meetings, presentations and speeches

provides ample means and opportunities for suggestions

provides a wide range of opportunities for feedback

makes effective use of feedback to solve problems before they become a crisis

makes effective use of feedback to avoid communication breakdowns

uses feedback to promote morale and trust

keeps well informed of feedback

investigates and promptly follows up on serious feedback issues

is skilled in following up on action-needed feedback

welcomes feedback at every opportunity

fosters a climate where dissent or criticism is accepted

encourages positive and negative feedback

FEEDBACK

welcomes both good and bad feedback

responds positively to unfavorable feedback

acts promptly on constructive feedback

is able to distinguish between valuable feedback and hearsay

excels in promoting unsolicited feedback

encourages honest feedback

is able to provide unfavorable feedback with suggestions for improvement

is continuously providing feedback for improvements

takes the initiative in providing valuable feedback

is very reliable in providing sound objective and effective feedback

is very reliable in providing accurate and timely feedback

is especially helpful in providing valuable feedback on new policies, programs, products, etc.

is skilled in keeping superiors well informed of valuable feedback

is gaining the attention of superiors for sound and objective feedback

is widely recognized for excellent feedback

GLOBAL

recognizes the growing value of a global presence

is fast adapting to increased globalization

recognizes the growing importance of global thinking

keeps well aware of global advancements, challenges, technologies and trends

is prepared to meet global challenges

maintains close communications with global operations

works well with global personnel and operations

keeps alert to global opportunities

is striving for a greater global presence

is fast increasing global capabilities

keeps well informed of global issues

is very knowable in global economics

closely follows global research

keeps well informed of global creativity and innovation

GOALS AND OBJECTIVES

effectively develops individual, departmental and organizational goals to attain objectives

effectively organizes, assembles and arranges resources to meet goals

seeks proper training to achieve goals

sets goals that are compatible with those of the organization

effectively blends personal goals with organizational objectives

sets high standards of personal performance

sets compelling personal goals

excels in forming goals and plans of action

establishes clear goals to achieve significant productive impact

establishes clear goals and purposes

sets realistic goals

establishes feasible and attainable goals

sets goals that are realistic, achievable and credible

establishes special and achievable goals

effectively develops goals

sets worthy goals

excels in setting annual and long-term performance goals

(continued)

GOALS AND OBJECTIVES

is able to modify goals based on changing situations

establishes special and measurable goals

effectively evaluates goals

is able to obtain broad support for achieving goals

keeps employees focused on achieving goals

provides incentives for achieving goals

establishes methods for attaining goals

uses goals to maintain momentum

effectively establishes group goals

is committed to shared goals

is aware of longer-term goals and larger framework of concepts

is a goal seeker

is an enthusiastic goal achiever

achieves and surpasses goals

excels in planning, forecasting, setting objectives and determining courses of action

encompasses every objective valued by the organization

sets, obtains and manages managerial objectives

sets innovative objectives

GOALS AND OBJECTIVES

sets clear and measurable objectives

formulates realistic objectives

effectively determines workable objectives

is able to successfully change objectives based on unforeseen circumstances

establishes special objectives

excels in the perception of objectives

effectively develops objectives

effectively communicates objectives

articulates clear objectives

achieves cognitive objectives

effectively sets group performance objectives

effectively establishes truly relevant objectives and performance standards

displays sincerity of ambitions and objectives

keeps focused on performance objectives

establishes performance targets for both short-range and long-range

effectively sets optimal targets

sets reachable targets

IMPROVEMENT

is a major contributor to organization improvement

is steadily improving the department's contribution to the organization

makes improvements for the benefit of the organization

strives to continuously improve policies, methods and procedures

develops continuous improvement methods

concentrates on improving core capabilities

builds on fundamental capabilities and strengths

strives to continuously strengthen and refine professional effectiveness

seeks higher levels of expertise

strives to improve performance

strives for personal enrichment

is continuously planning for improvement

is continuously searching for ways to improve

strives for continuous improvement

displays a strong drive for continuous improvement

focuses on continuous improvement

sustains continuous improvement

seeks continuous improvement

is committed to continuous improvement

makes effective use of educational and training programs to improve performance

is taking measures to improve performance

moves constructively toward improving performance

excels in enhancing performance

assigns a high priority to improving employee performance

focuses on improving employee performance

provides the resources needed to support employee improvement

recognizes and praises employee improvement

corrects shortcomings of subordinates

promotes improvement-oriented ideas

makes frequent and valuable suggestions for improvement

excels in developing improved techniques

improves effectiveness by eliminating the confusing

develops totally new strategies for improvement

devises improved means of accomplishing results

(continued)

IMPROVEMENT

produces changes for the overall improvement of the department

understands the need for improvement

displays a willingness to discuss weaknesses and make improvements

discusses in a tactful manner the areas in need of improvement

works cooperatively toward the identification of areas needing improvement

excels in isolating characteristics in need of improvement

identifies specific improvements to be achieved

pinpoints areas of needed improvement

focuses on areas having the greatest potential for improvement

excels in self-supervision and self-improvement

establishes goals for improvement of performance targets

develops future goals for self-improvement

sets ambitious growth goals

articulates goals for future improvement

identifies performance measurement problems

strives for higher levels of improvement

establishes clear expectations

IMPROVEMENT

monitors improvement progress

displays an eagerness to improve

demonstrates a strong effort to improve

seeks opportunities for self-improvement

welcomes opportunities for improvement

seeks feedback to improve performance

seeks advice for improving performance

uses constructive criticism to improve performance

responds favorably to suggested actions for improvement

displays improved potential for advancement

displays continuous improvement and consistent progress

is showing sustainable improvement

is showing exceptional improvement

shows steady progress

displays significant progress

shows sustained long-term growth

continues to grow and improve

INITIATIVE

demonstrates a high level of initiative

takes charge in the absence of detailed instructions

takes action without undue haste or delay

takes prompt and independent action

takes the initiative in developing new methods, procedures and approaches

is extremely active and eager to try new approaches

is eager to take on new projects

finds new and better ways of performing job

offers many unsought suggestions for improving efficiency

effectively applies new concepts and techniques

demonstrates an ability to think along constructive and original lines

is energetic and enterprising

is a self-starter

plans and organizes with little or no assistance

displays self-reliant enterprise

possesses the quality of knowing what has to be done

does things without being told

INITIATIVE

displays strong initiative in carrying out assignments

is judicious in carrying out assignments without direction

excels in self-directing and self-pacing

originates many successful programs

makes practical suggestions

displays ingenuity in anticipating and meeting unexpected situations

takes the initiative in solving problems

effectively initiates solutions

gathers and provides data in advance of need

excels in identifying new areas of opportunities

takes advantage of all opportunities

explores new opportunities

keeps alert to greater opportunities

is always alert for unique opportunities

provides opportunities for initiative

takes the initiative in expressing views during group discussions

requires minimum supervision

INNOVATION

instills innovation as a company-wide challenge

promotes a culture of innovation

is an innovative planner of new products and programs

innovates for future success

excels in developing innovative and creative solutions

seeks innovative solutions

develops innovative plans and solutions

creates innovative and distinctive programs

innovates and creates new and unique methods and procedures

promotes innovative thinking

excels in innovative thinking

excels in promoting innovative changes

excels in proposing innovative and practical ideas

is always searching for innovative ideas

is always willing to implement new ideas and approaches

is able to successfully overcome resistance to new ideas

takes innovative steps to achieve results

INNOVATION

is committed to continuous innovation

seeks continuous innovation

is continuously innovative

is continuously implementing innovative practices

fosters a curiosity for innovative possibilities

considers innovative possibilities

encourages innovation

promotes innovation

promotes value through innovation

displays strong innovative capabilities

displays innovative strategies

develops innovative approaches

is willing to undertake new and untested approaches

is skilled in developing imaginative new approaches

demonstrates innovative insight

is very innovative when confronted with limited resources

is extremely innovative under adverse conditions

INTELLECTUAL PROPERTY MGT.

is highly skilled in communicating to employees the importance of intellectual properties

is very effective in communicating the value of intellectual properties

excels in preparing and distributing policy statements concerning the proper application and identification of patents, trademarks and copyrights

ensures that employees strictly comply with the organization's intellectual property policies

ensures that employees recognize the need to protect intellectual properties

informs all new employees of the critical need to protect intellectual properties

excels in giving a high priority to intellectual property protection and remedies

takes appropriate measures to protect intellectual properties

is quick to aggressively defend intellectual property rights

protects proprietary rights with aggressive action

is willing to devote significant resources to defending patents, trademarks, copyrights and other intellectual property rights

is aggressive in protecting intellectual properties both domestically and internationally

INTELLECTUAL PROPERTY MGT.

possesses a strong knowledge of protecting
intellectual properties in a global economy

is skilled in submitting applications
and obtaining patents

monitors possible patent infringements
and takes action if needed

is very effective in stressing the value
of trademarks

is very reliable in scheduling and renewing
registered trademarks to prevent elapses

excels in continuously searching the
Internet for possible copyright infringements

takes prompt and aggressive action to
protect copyrighted material

excels in ensuring that employees recognize
the critical importance of protecting trade
secrets

is very effective in stressing the need to
protect formulas, ingredients, processes etc.

is very strict in preventing visitors from entering
restricted areas containing secret materials,
machines and processes

effectively controls the proper release of
proprietary information

displays good judgment in referring all inquires
on intellectual properties to management

keeps alert to counterfeiting and piracy of
intellectual properties

INTERPERSONAL SKILLS

displays talent, enthusiasm and commitment

displays a high degree of recognition, acceptance and prestige in dealing with others

makes favorable impression and easily gains acceptance by others

identifies and understands personal values of superiors, subordinates, peers and others

displays genuineness in dealing with others

is very tactful in relationships with others

recognizes the needs of others

is well accepted by others under difficult circumstances

demonstrates strong interpersonal skills

displays an interpersonal regard

makes excellent first impressions

recognizes the importance of first impressions

projects a pleasant demeanor

is quick to earn the respect of others

is quick to gain recognition and respect

is able to quickly establish rapport

builds a close rapport

builds trust and rapport

builds a climate of trust

INTERPERSONAL SKILLS

excels in trust building

promotes relationships of trust and respect

develops interpersonal trust

develops relationships based on dependability and honesty

understands human behavior

excels in effective human relations

builds on mutual dependence and understanding

understands and knows how to get along with co-workers

develops mutual support

establishes effective working relationships

develops positive working relationships

works effectively with other divisions and departments

works effectively with both new and experienced employees

promotes harmony among associates

attracts the favorable attention of superiors

builds positive relationships with superiors

works effectively with multiple superiors

conveys considerable influence with superiors

(continued)

INTERPERSONAL SKILLS

establishes credibility with superiors
and subordinates

gains management commitments

excels in obtaining enthusiastic commitments

interacts effectively with peers

displays unconditional positive regard

exercises considerable influence

conveys positive influences

displays positive traits

conveys a positive personal image

conveys a willingness to help

generates synergy

promotes participative approaches

demonstrates an ability to relate

makes effective use of humor in tense
situations

excels in sustaining concentration while
avoiding confrontations

demonstrates strong listening skills

respects the opinions of others

makes wise and fair judgments based on solid facts

uses sound judgment based on broad experiences

is reliable in using good judgment

is very open-minded in judgmental situations

is open-minded when forming opinions

gives thoughtful consideration before forming opinions

forms opinions based on sound judgment

excels in making appropriate judgments

makes thoughtful determinations

displays excellent intuitive judgment

follows a disciplined approach when forming judgments

exercises careful deliberations before making judgments

weighs alternative courses of action

valuates options in terms of consequences

effectively diagnoses situations or conditions

is not governed by conventional wisdom

exercises sound judgment on behalf of others

KNOWLEDGE

is well informed of critical issues affecting the organization

knows basic management principles and methods

possesses the knowledge to handle work of the most complex nature

understands the purposes, objectives, practices and procedures of the department

understands thoroughly all aspects of job

understands needs and requirements of job

possesses an intrinsic knowledge of the job

is secure in job knowledge

is very knowledgeable over a wide range of job responsibilities

displays a strong knowledge of responsibilities

demonstrates a strong, functional knowledge of position

displays a broad application of knowledge

is able to effectively apply knowledge

effectively applies educational background

excels in the dissemination of knowledge

excels in conveying knowledge to others

shares knowledge for the benefit of employees

KNOWLEDGE

displays a strong understanding of current and relevant issues

keeps alert to current practices

demonstrates a comprehensive knowledge of the field

is highly regarded for knowledge of the field

keeps abreast of the latest thinking in the field

keeps informed of emerging issues in the field

is well informed of the latest ideas, trends and predictions in the field

keeps informed of the latest trends and developments

is expanding knowledge to encompass a global perspective

possesses a working knowledge of several languages

keeps well informed of business, political and social issues

keeps well informed of the business environment

keeps fully abreast of changing government regulations

keeps well informed of pertinent legislation and regulations

is exceptionally well informed

(continued)

KNOWLEDGE

is a preeminent authority

possesses broad experience

displays a strong depth of experience

possesses a proven record of successful experience

possesses an extraordinary level of experience

possesses practical hands-on experience

demonstrates excellent "real world" experience

recognizes the power of information

is a trusted resource for information

possesses an invaluable source of knowledge

provides educational resources for improving knowledge

is continuously strengthening knowledge-building resources

is eager to participate in seminars and all knowledge-building activities

is continuously attending seminars and conferences to maintain professional expertise

encourages employees to take advantages of all educational opportunities

excels in gaining knowledge through continuous study

projects self-confidence, authority and enthusiasm

displays the confidence needed to face the toughest leadership challenges

is successfully meeting the position's leadership challenges

faces problems with confidence and assurance

maintains a high profile in the organization

displays a high level of leadership experience

demonstrates natural leadership ability

demonstrates decisive leadership ability

displays a strong ability to lead and direct

displays leadership stature

demonstrates strong, dynamic leadership

shows dynamic leadership qualities

is a charismatic leader

displays the strengths of the exceptional leader

is widely recognized as a strong leader

demonstrates excellence in a critical leadership role

demonstrates imaginative leadership

is willing to challenge conventional wisdom

(continued)

LEADERSHIP

provides critical leadership

displays many leadership competencies

demonstrates core leadership skills

possesses key leadership characteristics

displays leadership traits appropriate to the situation

conveys an authoritative image that commands respect

commands a high degree of influence

effectively uses power and influence

knows when to restrain and when to exercise power

is very effective in asserting leadership abilities

is able to assert authority when challenged

radiates authority

leads with authority and respect

inspires confidence and respect

commands the respect of others

radiates confidence

inspires distinguished performance

is an inspirational leader

is motivating and inspiring

LEADERSHIP

takes a leadership role in group situations

displays a high degree of courage

effectively maintains leadership in a group environment

is emulated by peers and subordinates

displays a strong ability to build credibility

earns the respect and loyalty of subordinates

inspires trust and confidence

is a trusted leader

is quick to gain the trust of others

commands undivided attention

excels in training, leading and motivating people

is able to quickly create rapport

is able to quickly gain the support of others

inspires others to do their best

shows appreciation for contributions and achievements

promotes a high degree of morale

promotes harmony and teamwork

creates shared drive and purpose

LEARNING SKILLS

shows eagerness and capacity to learn

displays exceptional learning capacity

responds quickly to new instructions, situations, methods and procedures

displays an exceptional ability to learn new methods

is quick to learn the operation of new computers, equipment and machines

is quick to learn new methods, procedures and techniques

displays an ability to learn rapidly and adapt quickly to changing situations

is able to quickly grasp new routines and explanations

responds promptly to changes and opportunities

displays a short learning curve

is a fast learner

views new duties and projects as a learning experience

keeps alert to new learning opportunities

takes advantage of all learning opportunities

welcomes all learning opportunities

is receptive to new ideas

uses sound techniques to maximize learning

LEARNING SKILLS

makes effective use of hands-on learning

is eager to learn new methods, techniques and approaches

is always eager to learn new skills

is very enthusiastic about learning new skills

is eager to enhance skill levels

makes a strong effort to maintain new skills

learns quickly from setbacks

learns from mistakes and past actions

benefits from all learning situations

is able to learn and teach other employees

shares learning experience with subordinates

creates a stimulating learning environment

encourages a positive learning environment

promotes a learning climate

stimulates curiosity to improve learning

is committed to continuous learning

is continuously learning through educational and professional improvement programs

LOGISTICS

ensures the successful coordination of complex operations covering the flow of information and materials from their point of origin to their final consumption or usage

closely monitors every level of logistics from raw materials to final delivery

is very knowledgeable of both global and domestic logistical advancements

is continuously improving our logistical capabilities

keeps abreast of the latest developments in supply chain automation

uses artificial intelligence to increase efficiencies at every level of our supply chain

takes immediate action to correct any weaknesses in the supply chain

is continuously monitoring our supply chain to prevent interruptions and breakdowns

continuously monitors vendor performance to ensure highly reliable and efficient logistics

is continuously monitoring logistical costs to achieve optimal efficiency

recognizes the importance of maintaining sufficient inventories to provide reliable logistics support

takes prompt alternative actions to meet critical supply needs

excels in providing prompt logistics in areas recovering from natural disasters

LOYALTY AND DEDICATION

places a high priority on loyalty and dedication

encourages loyalty throughout the organization

is a strong supporter of all organizational programs and activities

is loyal in supporting the organization's community activities

displays strong loyalty to superiors and to the organization

is loyal to organization, associates and subordinates

is highly committed to achieving organizational success

shows concern for the welfare and success of the organization

displays a genuine interest in the organization

is committed to organizational goals

takes pride in contributing to the organization's success

builds loyalty in subordinates

shows positive attitudes toward employer and employees

encourages employee pride and loyalty

increases superior's strengths

builds loyalty at every opportunity

(continued)

LOYALTY AND DEDICATION

expects strong loyalty

displays a high degree of honesty, loyalty and integrity

displays loyalty to profession

takes pride in job

is a highly dedicated employee

is a highly dedicated professional

is extremely dedicated

demonstrates untiring dedication

displays unwavering dedication

displays a strong spirit of dedication

is totally committed to achieving excellence

is highly devoted to achieving objectives

demonstrates an unparalleled commitment

is committed to a sustained long-term success

projects a renewed sense of purpose

demonstrates a continuous and diligent effort

demonstrates a high level of loyal commitment

MAINTENANCE MANAGEMENT

excels in managing maintenance operations

develops excellent routine maintenance programs

develops strong preventive maintenance measures

is highly skilled in developing sound maintenance schedules using artificial intelligence

demonstrates a strong awareness of the economic importance of lost production time

is able to keep production down-time to a minimum

excels in planning major maintenance projects during plant shut-downs

is highly skilled in preventing major equipment break-downs

takes prompt actions to prevent minor maintenance problems from becoming major concerns

is continuously inspecting machinery for signs of wear

is quick to repair sudden break-downs

is very accurate in forecasting the life-expectancy of major equipment

excels in keeping management informed of anticipated expenditures for machinery replacement

(continued)

MAINTENANCE MANAGEMENT

demonstrates a strong ability to control maintenance costs

develops sound and realistic maintenance budgets

is able to minimize overtime

maintains excellent relationships with technical support personnel of machinery manufacturers

is skilled in maintaining highly technical and sophisticated manufacturing machinery

works effectively with machinery suppliers to ensure proper maintenance

works closely with engineering personnel to solve maintenance problems

is extremely knowledgeable in knowing whether to repair or replace a component

is very accurate in predicting repair time

keeps very accurate and current maintenance records

makes effective use of maintenance software

excels in all areas of professional facility maintenance

is very professional in maintaining an attractive facility with well kept grounds

MAINTENANCE MANAGEMENT

recognizes that an attractive work environment contributes to high employee morale

works effectively with human resources to ensure the hiring of qualified maintenance personnel

is skilled in training new personnel in order to ensure a continuous knowledge of unique repair situations

makes effective use of mentoring to develop maintenance skills

conducts continuous training to improve departmental effectiveness

is very professional in conducting maintenance training sessions

makes effective use of videos to train maintenance personnel

works effectively with purchasing personnel to obtain high quality maintenance supplies consistent with cost considerations

is very effective in managing inventories of maintenance supplies

keeps maintenance storage areas neat and orderly

places a high priority on maintenance worker safety

keeps well informed of safety and environmental issues

MANAGEMENT SKILLS - TOP MGT.

is able to sustain organizational success in
a highly competitive environment

keeps the organization well positioned to
meet future challenges

is strategically positioning the organization
to achieve future success

develops strategic plans to ensure the
organization's future success

plans effectively for the long-term
success of the organization

keeps fully alert to the weaknesses,
strengths, threats and opportunities
facing the organization

strives to place the organization in
a premier position

excels in achieving long-term sustainable
growth

excels in creating long-term shareholder
value

is skilled in formulating a grand vision

is effective in communicating the organization's
mission, values and strategies

builds a corporate culture committed
to excellence

obtains full commitments throughout
the organization

pulls the organization together

MANAGEMENT SKILLS - TOP MGT.

builds organizational harmony

effectively solves problems that cross
organization boundaries

effectively recognizes the need for change

provides a stabilizing influence during
periods of organizational change

possesses high-level management experience

demonstrates superior executive ability
under a variety of circumstances

demonstrates an ability to recognize
management problems and develop solutions

is a polished and effective executive

conveys executive stature

conveys an executive presence

displays executive strength

displays sound ethics

maintains high ethical standards

is highly respected in the industry

manages resources to achieve competitive
advantages

excels in the strategic repositioning
of company resources

effectively integrates objectives, resources
and opportunities

(continued)

MANAGEMENT SKILLS - TOP MGT.

builds strong support of organizational objectives

is always searching for new revenue streams

takes strong measures to increase potential for revenue enhancements

excels in generating revenue growth

keeps alert to global opportunities

is fast adapting to increased globalization

ensures that all policies are accurate, thoroughly documented and consistently applied

effectively oversees fiduciary responsibilities

gives a high priority to corporate governance principles

is well informed of legislative and regulatory activities affecting the organization

keeps alert to all measures that will avoid organizational liability

is effective in taking measures to reduce the organization's exposure to litigation

is very effective in communicating outside the organization

builds and reinforces major programs with strong success

orchestrates successful management-driven programs

MANAGEMENT SKILLS - TOP MGT.

develops strong and successful company-wide programs

identifies major management problems

deals promptly and effectively with adverse developments

knows when to seek outside consultants

is able to accurately assess management effectiveness

displays strengths in human resources management

excels in human capital management

excels in developing synergistic strategies

excels in developing employee retention programs

is highly respected by lower level management

keeps well informed of executive committee activities

maintains close contact with key executives

gives close attention to successor management

devotes proper attention to executive successor programs

MANAGEMENT SKILLS - MIDDLE MGT.

displays attributes of an effective manager

is a challenging and inspiring manager

displays an effective, productive management style

recognizes the difference between managing and doing

shows those qualities that make a manager forceful and effective

effectively applies sound management principles

effectively follows contemporary management approaches

follows prudent management practices

demonstrates productive management skills

displays management efficiency and effectiveness

encourages participative management

is a powerful asset to the organization

multiplies management effectiveness

is continuously striving to improve department efficiency and effectiveness

ensures that operations run efficiently and economically

provides subordinates with the resources needed to attain results

MANAGEMENT SKILLS - MIDDLE MGT.

attains results through the proper direction of subordinates

gives clear directions

keeps subordinates motivated

achieves high productive output while maintaining high morale

excels in defining, measuring and increasing productivity

is able to maintain high productivity with a limited staff

sets realistic and measurable department goals

recognizes the important roles of responsibility, authority and accountability

avoids overstepping authority

establishes accountability throughout the department

holds subordinates accountable for results

demands accountability from subordinates

accounts for effective and efficient use of personnel

excels in solving people problems

adheres to all policies, procedures and rules of decorum

follows proper codes of conduct

(continued)

MANAGEMENT SKILLS - MIDDLE MGT.

effectively enforces policies, rules and regulations

enforces strict conformance to written policies and guidelines

is able to strictly enforce unpopular decisions

is well trained in crisis management

avoids managing by crisis

respects both employee rights and management prerogatives

effectively resolves conflicts between individual needs and requirements of the organization

demonstrates an ability to overcome internal barriers

maintains firm departmental control

obtains the full support of other departments

excels in resolving interdepartmental conflicts

develops a cohesive department effort

achieves a high degree of teamwork within the department

encourages efforts toward common goals

manages change effectively

implements changes with minimal resistance

deals effectively with resistance to change

MANAGEMENT SKILLS - MIDDLE MGT.

implements change with a positive impact

is able to implement change in a reluctant environment

is able to break through barriers of resistance when implementing changes

excels in obtaining top management support

keeps top management informed on questions of policy

prepares consistent and appropriate recommendations

excels in human resources management

provides top management with valid and reliable information for human resources planning

excels in managing distant employees

effectively manages employees at satellite locations

keeps off site employees fully informed of all plans, actions and developments

effectively manages self

shows strong self-management

keeps employees aware of their importance to the organization

MATURITY

displays a high degree of emotional maturity

keeps situations in proper perspective

excels in separating emotion from rationality

displays emotional stability

displays strong emotional control

avoids emotional involvement

copes constructively with emotions

avoids overreacting

keeps anger under control

confronts reality

displays mature reactions

maintains a mature attitude

maintains strong self-control

displays superior emotional adjustments
and stability

recovers promptly from unfortunate
circumstances

displays maturity in handling disappointments

responds positively on inconsequential issues

takes the initiative in expressing views during staff meetings

performs an active role in meetings

makes a strong impact at meetings

commands respect as a skilled meeting participant

schedules meetings only when necessary

makes effective use of meetings to motivate and train

uses meetings to effectively provide information on important issues

ensures that all attendees are in a position to contribute or benefit from discussions

prepares well defined meeting agendas

distributes agendas well in advance of meetings

follows-up on previous meeting action plans and results

encourages active participation in all meetings

keeps meetings on subject, productive and on schedule

keeps meetings action-oriented

excels in preparing accurate meeting minutes with clear action plans and assignments

MENTAL SKILLS

grasps the most difficult concepts

displays a depth of understanding

understands both theoretical and practical concepts

excels in both theoretical and practical thinking

is capable of preparing highly complex statistical data

excels in making accurate mental calculations

is exceptionally keen and alert

is reasonable, smart and keen

is alert, quick and responsive

is alert and broad-minded

keeps alert to strategic opportunities

is capable of sustaining a high level of concentration

is able to focus on a single task until completion

gives undivided attention

is not governed by conventional thinking

assesses assumptions and methodologies on a continuous basis

is quick to question underlying assumptions

is continuously rethinking traditional assumptions

MENTAL SKILLS

demonstrates original and independent thinking

displays logical thought patterns

follows logical thinking patterns

sustains logical thinking in one area

uses sound logic to arrive at conclusions

displays a consistent and systematic thinking process

thinks before taking action

thinks fast on feet

uses common sense

uses common sense to reach workable conclusions

draws sound conclusions

uses sound fact-finding approaches

displays fresh insights

is skilled in developing practical insights

uses intelligent reasoning

demonstrates sound inductive and deductive reasoning

displays strong mental flexibility

exhibits mental toughness when necessary

(continued)

MENTAL SKILLS

displays critical thinking

displays fresh thinking

displays imaginative thinking

displays organized thinking

excels in intuitive thinking

excels in divergent thinking

excels in heuristic thinking

excels in independent thinking

thinks futuristically

thinks strategically

displays consistent, logical and orderly thinking

displays excellent comprehension and retention

displays a high level of knowledge retention

displays strong powers of mental retention

excels in retaining and recalling information

possesses strong memory skills

displays strong memory power

possesses a strong ability to remember and recall

displays a remarkable power to remember details

MENTAL SKILLS

possesses multilingual skills

is able to understand and speak in other languages

displays a very high cognitive ability

excels in systematic observation

displays strong powers of observation

displays diverse perspectives

gains new and broad perspectives

distinguishes between perception and reality

demonstrates intellectual inquisitiveness

displays an inquiring mind

widens intellectual horizons

makes effective use of mental imaging

possesses strong visionary powers

makes very accurate predictions

is able to foresee approaching problems

demonstrates positive mental outlook

is a positive thinker

recognizes the growing importance of global thinking

MOTIVATION

is strongly motivated to achieve higher expectations

is strongly motivated to achieve optimal results

displays a strong incentive to succeed

is highly motivated to achieve individual attainment

strives for the achievement of excellence

strives for excellence at every opportunity

is committed to excellence

strives for maximum effectiveness

is very performance conscious

displays energy and vitality in performing daily responsibilities

displays maximum drive fulfilling job responsibilities

displays a relentless drive to perform

displays high energy and drive

displays strong achievement drive

is a significant driving force

keeps drive alive

displays highly motivated inner drive

displays a strong sense of purpose

MOTIVATION

remains highly committed

displays a sustained commitment

displays a strong personal commitment

demonstrates a high level of commitment

is highly committed to achieving strong future performance

displays a strong competitive drive

provides a competitive edge

turns competitive impulses into the most constructive channels

displays intense desire

demonstrates strong will power and determination

optimizes individual traits

is ambitious and high-spirited

displays an enthusiastic spirit

displays a spirit of determination

is realistically enthusiastic

maintains fresh enthusiasm

displays energy and enthusiasm

works with enthusiasm

displays extraordinary enthusiasm

(continued)

MOTIVATION

generates enthusiasm

inspires enthusiasm

builds enthusiasm for ideas

is a powerful motivational speaker

is able to highly motivate others

builds employee enthusiasm

develops a motivating environment

instills energy and enthusiasm

motivates and challenges

seeks greater challenges

welcomes exciting challenges

thrives on challenges

accentuates the positive

generates positive attitudes

maintains a positive attitude

provides positive reinforcements
to achieve results

uses positive reinforcement to motivate

displays positive energy

maintains a high energy level

is highly energized

MOTIVATION

is highly energetic and enterprising

goes beyond what is expected

gives maximum effort

displays intense involvement

seeks total involvement

volunteers for extra work and demanding challenges

is totally absorbed in job

strives for sustainable success

is success-oriented

is compelled to succeed

is quick to identify opportunities

capitalizes on opportunities

views problems as opportunities

maximizes opportunities with every situation

operates effectively under adverse conditions

recoils promptly from problems

turns past failures into future successes

effectively overcomes personal and organizational blocks to achieve results

maximizes all resources to achieve results

(continued)

MOTIVATION

looks beyond obstacles

surpasses obstacles

is able to overcome extreme difficulties

is a prime mover

is a compulsive achiever

is ambitious and hard-driving

is persistent in achieving goals

is task-oriented

is achievement-oriented

is results-oriented

is results-driven

displays progressive attributes

is seldom complacent

is not content with mediocrity

is a self-motivator

maintains self-motivation

maintains own momentum

sustains a high level of momentum

is an enthusiastic supporter of all programs

makes effective use of positive imagery to
achieve success

MULTI-TASKING

is highly skilled in simultaneously performing a wide range of mental and physical tasks

is very proficient in simultaneously handling divergent tasks

excels in simultaneously performing a broad range of responsibilities

demonstrates a strong ability to simultaneously perform multiple tasks

possesses strong multi-tasking skills

is skilled in communicating verbally while performing multiple tasks

makes a valuable contribution to the department using powerful multi-tasking skills

is very effective in using multi-tasking to maintain a steady flow of department operations

is very valuable in multi-tasking during times of employee absences and shortages

is able to maintain a high degree of productivity by multi-tasking

makes effective use of strong multi-tasking skills to achieve productive results

maintains a calm composure when facing multiple tasks and deadlines

is very efficient in multi-tasking especially in stressful situations

NEGOTIATING SKILLS

is consistently able to negotiate successful outcomes

is skilled in reaching mutual agreements

is able to reach mutual understandings

demonstrates strong negotiating skills

is widely recognized as a skilled negotiator

excels in negotiating fair resolutions

negotiates with skill

negotiates with tact

displays strength in negotiating

is an adept negotiator

possesses strong facilitation skills

is skilled as a key facilitator

effectively resolves misunderstandings

keeps conflicts from rising

anticipates and resolves conflicts

excels in resolving conflicts

displays strong conflict resolution skills

presents different opinions without creating conflicts

reconciles differences without creating resentment

NEGOTIATING SKILLS

works well with others in the solution of mutual problems

effectively handles differing viewpoints

is able to achieve coordination among various viewpoints

disagrees diplomatically

disagrees without arguing

is skilled in refusing unreasonable demands

knows how and when to say "no"

confronts issues in a timely and effective manner

is able to successfully confront when necessary

handles confrontations with tact

handles confrontations with skill

is extremely confident in facing confrontations

keeps assertiveness and empathy in balance when negotiating

prepares thoroughly for negotiations

makes effective use of timing in negotiations

excels in negotiating and documenting agreements

ORAL EXPRESSION

is a polished and confident speaker

is an eloquent speaker

is a formidable speaker

speaks with authority

is a forceful speaker

is an inspiring speaker

is able to inspire audiences

excels in speaking on special occasions

excels in impromptu speaking situations

excels in delivering impromptu remarks

excels in extemporaneous speaking

speaks effectively on feet

communicates with ease and a natural style

is a powerful communicator in group settings

conveys stature when speaking

makes effective demonstrations

makes effective use of questions

makes effective use of an extensive vocabulary

possesses superior verbal understanding

uses understandable language that is relevant and meaningful

ORAL EXPRESSION

uses concise and clear language

excels in speech proficiency

is proficient in pronunciation

is eminently clear in verbal expressions

is highly articulate

displays clarity in expressing views

states positions clearly

presents clear views and ideas

displays an ability to present views logically

is able to clearly express complicated issues in simple terms

expresses ideas clearly

speaks at a pleasant tempo

enunciates clearly in a well-modulated voice

speaks in a positive tone

speaks with enthusiasm and confidence

makes dynamic impressions

creates powerful and lasting impressions

ORGANIZING

develops programs to improve the effectiveness of the department and overall operation of the organization

effectively develops organizational capabilities and integration of objectives

continues to optimize organizational effectiveness

builds organizational effectiveness

exerts a positive influence on the organizational climate

deals effectively with organizational climate

is a major contributor to the strength and vitality of the organization

displays a broad grasp of the organization

identifies organizational needs

excels in developing jobs, organizational structures and systems

keeps organizational charts current

ensures that all responsibilities and functions are clearly defined

respects organizational levels of authority

encourages accountability throughout the organization

keeps organizational levels to a minimum

ORGANIZING

excels in minimizing the number of
organizational layers

avoids over-staffing

maximizes organizational productivity

makes a substantial contribution to the growth
of the organization

makes the most of organizational energy and
potential

excels in streamlining operations

overcomes organizational block-ups

is methodical in planning, organizing
and informing

makes order out of chaos

excels in turning chaos into order

excels in cutting through confusion

is neat and orderly

is very orderly and systematic

organizes effectively to achieve greater results

organizes work well

displays an organized approach to the job

PERSONAL QUALITIES

demonstrates a high degree of integrity, challenge and drive

possesses many valued personal traits

possesses all traits associated with excellence

is fair, cheerful and follows businesslike procedures to accomplish results

makes strong impressions

is very charismatic

displays a pleasant, cheerful disposition

displays natural charm and charisma

displays a pleasant demeanor

displays a calm, even temperament

is stable, patient and steady

is relaxed, confident and enjoyable

is very cordial

is polished and poised

displays social grace

is warm and genuine

is sincere

is serious minded

projects objectivity

PERSONAL QUALITIES

displays many positive character traits

displays refinement and character

is very energized and optimistic

maintains a positive outlook

remains optimistic under adverse conditions

is highly resilient

views problems as opportunities

maintains a sense of humor

uses humor constructively

is quick to build rapport

makes a dynamic presence

is highly respected

is very punctual

is efficient and effective

displays impeccable honestly and trust

shows a keen wit

is always willing to assist others

is a strong participant in company sponsored community activities

is highly credible

is highly regarded for personal credibility

(continued)

PERSONAL QUALITIES

is very trustworthy

demonstrate integrity that is beyond reproach

is highly regarded for integrity

displays character and integrity

maintains high recognition

demonstrates a commitment to core values

remains steadfast to core beliefs

displays a remarkable strength of conviction

is self-reliant

is able to strongly focus efforts

is highly focused

recognizes and accepts personal assets and liabilities

recognizes personal limitations

displays many action-oriented skills

projects energy and enthusiasm

is highly talented, trained and committed

PERSUASIVENESS

demonstrates strong persuasive powers

demonstrates strong persuasive skills

demonstrates excellent persuasive ability

uses chronological reasoning to effectively persuade

uses sound reasoning to effectively persuade

excels in using logical thinking to persuade

effectively persuades using strong arguments

excels in acquiring support for decisions and actions

is very successful in using persuasion to obtain approvals

is very skilled in gaining the support of others

is a strong consensus-builder

is very effective in gaining support for a consensus

excels in gaining support of views and opinions

is able to change the views of others without causing resentment

is able to gain the acceptance of views and positions

excels in changing attitudes

reinforces ideas and proposals with sound documentation

(continued)

PERSUASIVENESS

is successful in overcoming negativity
and resistance

is very effective in overcoming objections using
skillful persuasion

is able to consistently overcome objections and
reach common agreements

persuades without antagonizing

persuades with tact

persuades with enthusiasm

seeks persuasive challenges

makes persuasive presentations

makes effective use of visual aids to persuade

communicates with persuasion

is a polished and persuasive communicator

makes memorable and convincing impressions

is very convincing

is very influential

conveys a strong influence

uses voice and body to effectively convince
and persuade

excels in both short-range and long-range planning

develops sound action plans

excels in developing tactical action plans

develops workable action plans

develops sound contingency plans

translates planning into reality

effectively translates ideas into action

effectively puts plans into action

is very skilled in turning theory into action

makes strategically sound plans

formulates sound strategies

develops rational planning strategies

develops effective strategies to attain good performance

plans unique and effective strategies

develops techniques to generate new strategic alternatives

excels in developing strategic alternatives

develops comprehensive strategies

develops positive strategies

excels in developing strategic aims

(continued)

PLANNING

excels in strategy and action

excels in formulating and executing strategies

is skilled in formulating and implementing strategic plans

excels in anticipatory management

excels in anticipating approaching problems and opportunities

creates flexible plans to meet changing opportunities

anticipates emerging opportunities

excels in anticipating reactions

excels in anticipating needs

is adept at assessing needs

excels in planning, forecasting and replenishing vital needs

makes accurate assessments of needs

plans effectively to make maximum use of all resources

excels in projecting resource needs

excels in logistical planning

plans effectively to meet peak demands

is highly proficient in scheduling materials, labor and operations

PLANNING

uses sound planning to maintain critical inventory levels

plans effectively to maintain a steady work flow

effectively plans to avoid future problems

prevents problems from occurring

excels in problem prevention

plans effectively to meet approaching problems

is very competent in emergency planning management

excels in crisis prevention

plans for the unexpected

plans effectively for uncertain conditions

anticipates and plans for changes

plans for repercussions of changes

excels in developing "what if" scenarios

plans for predictable resistance

plans for negative reactions

plans for success

is quick to recognize emerging trends

plans effectively for future development

focuses on the future

POTENTIAL

possesses the knowledge, experience and leadership qualities to achieve success at a higher management level

displays high management potential

possesses a strong capacity to make a greater contribution to the organization

is a strong contender for a higher position

is capable of distinguished performance in a higher level position

is a high potential employee with broad and solid experience

is a high potential employee with proven skills

is strongly qualified for advancement

is a strong candidate for advancement

displays strong potential for advancement

is uniquely positioned for advancement

is reaching the level for promotional consideration

is highly promotable

is underutilizing skills and is promotable to a higher level of responsibility

is outgrowing present position

is over qualified for present position

is capable of assuming greater challenges

POTENTIAL

is ready for a greater challenge

is eager for a career advancement

is capable of handling bigger projects and assignments

is qualified for greater responsibility

is presently capable of assuming greater responsibility

is capable of managing a larger department

is capable of assuming a greater leadership role

shows strong potential

displays a high energy potential

turns potential into action

possesses many latent strengths

displays a strong capacity for growth

is capably meeting the challenge of continuous growth

is capable of assuming greater responsibility in present position

is able to achieve ample opportunity for growth in present position

needs more responsibility to ensure continuous satisfaction and career growth

(continued)

POTENTIAL

is gradually being assigned increased
responsibilities to improve advancement
potential

is highly motivated for greater opportunities

is eager to demonstrate greater potential

displays a strong desire for advancement

is continuously seeking greater responsibility

is eager to assume greater responsibility in the
department or elsewhere

keeps alert to potential opportunities

seeks enhanced opportunities for growth

is making a strong effort to acquire greater
experience and skills to increase potential for
advancement

is enhancing growth potential through
additional education and training

excels in identifying and evaluating high
potential employees

encourages all employees to develop to their
fullest potential

takes pride in developing subordinates
for promotion

keeps management informed of employees
with strong growth potential

PRESENTATION SKILLS

demonstrates excellent oral presentation skills

demonstrates strong personal presentation skills

is a skillful presenter

is a convincing presenter

is a professional presenter

is a recognized and highly regarded presenter

makes presentations with poise and confidence

makes presentations with care and style

delivers presentations with enthusiasm and energy

makes lively and effective presentations

makes presentations that are interesting and lively

makes impressive presentations

creates indelible impressions when making presentations

delivers presentations with maximum impact

makes presentations that deliver a powerful message

makes powerful presentations

prepares persuasive presentations

makes effective use of body language

(continued)

139

PRESENTATION SKILLS

makes outstanding presentations to management

excels in making presentations to management that receive approval

promotes an excellent image when making presentations to groups outside the organization

faces any size audience with confidence

is able to gain the respect of audiences

is skilled in capturing the interests and involvement of audiences

is skilled in engaging audience participation

excels in directing audience participation

responds effectively to difficult questions and opposing views

handles unanticipated questions with skill

effectively organizes ideas for logical presentation and acceptance

communicates effectively with well designed materials

delivers well prepared presentations

makes presentations that are well researched and highly credible

is very skilled in preparing cost effective in-house presentations

PRESENTATION SKILLS

makes presentations that are visually compelling

uses visual aids effectively

makes effective use of charts, graphs, figures and illustrations

makes very effective use of words and graphics for maximum impact

creates visually impressive graphs and charts

excels in making powerful presentations using computer graphics

excels in developing and using computer generated presentations

is very skilled in making excellent use of presentation software

is skilled in making presentations for video recordings

makes excellent live presentations in video conferences

is able to effectively present dry and technical information

excels in presenting complex information and technical data

is able to present complex information in a simple format

strives continuously to improve presentation skills

PRIORITIZING

is able to successfully prioritize when
faced with requests, demands and deadlines

displays a strong sense of priorities

keeps situations in proper perspective

keeps priorities in proper sequence

excels in priority determinations

excels in prioritizing objectives

excels in priority management

conveys priority status when assigning duties
and projects

allocates sufficient resources to high
priority projects

gives full support to high priority projects

focuses energies on high priority projects

places high priority projects on a special
assignment basis

effectively executes strategic priorities

effectively establishes task priorities

effectively schedules critical tasks

keeps focused on relevant policy issues

is able to capably prioritize the demands of
multiple superiors

PRIORITIZING

effectively copes with competing priorities

effectively handles competing priorities

meets logically developed priorities

concentrates on activities with a high payoff

focuses efforts in areas with the highest payoffs

concentrates on activities with the greatest payback

focuses on relevant issues

focuses on essential activities

focuses time and energy on meaningful activities

focuses effectively on critical aspects of the job

recognizes the difference between important and urgent

is able to recognize issues of critical importance

distinguishes between low and high priority activities

focuses on value-added activities

effectively distinguishes between value and non-value activities

excels in eliminating all activities not creating value

(continued)

PRIORITIZING

is able to distinguish between the crucial and trivial

identifies unessential activities

excels in eliminating unproductive activities

eliminates tasks which contribute the least to organizational goals

avoids useless trivia

is not burdened by details

sees the big picture

devotes appropriate time to strategic areas of importance

effectively prioritizes daily and weekly activities

gives prompt attention to urgent priorities

recognizes the need to concentrate on high priority assignments

effectively allocates time in relation to priorities

gives proper attention to monitoring the status of high priority projects

keeps priority projects on schedule

is skilled in completing priority projects on time

schedules priorities to meet deadlines

places organizational needs ahead of personal convenience

PROBLEM SOLVING

demonstrates a strong ability to identify, analyze and solve problems

develops cohesive solutions that benefit the entire organization

creates satisfying solutions in conformance with organizational policies

displays an ability to solve problems, think, reason and learn

follows a disciplined and consistent approach to problem solving

approaches problems from multiple points of view

follows diverse approaches to solving problems

uses a variety of methodologies in solving problems

uses the latest technologies to improve operations and overcome problems

is willing to utilize highly sophisticated computer models to solve difficult problems

uses sound analytical reasoning to solve difficult problems

applies sound logic to problem solving

displays a practical approach to solving problems

makes effective use of all organizational resources to solve problems

(continued)

PROBLEM SOLVING

knows when to seek outside advice when solving problems

is unusually decisive in handling problems

effectively solves problems rather than symptoms

keeps management informed of emerging problems

keeps informed of developing problems

gives sufficient attention to both short-term and long-term problems

focuses on core problems

excels in creative problem solving

excels in solving critical problems

shows a strong ability to solve problems

solves difficult problems with confidence

excels in solving multi-faceted problems

solves problems before they become critical

effectively solves problems at early stages

encourages subordinates to solve minor problems

is quick to identify problems

excels in identifying real problems

is skilled in identifying and solving bottlenecks

PROBLEM SOLVING

keeps problems in perspective

solves problems in order of priority

is respected for inventive approaches and ingenious solutions

develops non-traditional solutions

excels in developing viable solutions

is quick to resolve and overcome obstacles

excels in trouble shooting

considers all options in developing solutions

is skilled in proposing optional solutions

excels in developing alternative solutions

excels in developing real-world solutions

develops creative and cost effective solutions

develops satisfying solutions

makes a strong effort to be a part of the solution

works well with others in solving problems

welcomes suggestions for problem solving

translates problems into practical solutions

looks upon problems as exciting challenges

turns problems into opportunities

PRODUCTIVITY

makes a substantial contribution to the continued operation and growth of the organization

is an important contributor to the success of the department

is a proven performer

demonstrates consistent and distinguished performance

continues to maximize performance through increased efficiency

performs at peak efficiency

maintains a peak performance

sustains a high achievement level

works at a high achievement level

performs at a high energy level

effectively expends energy

maintains unusually high output

performs with unusual speed at a high rate of output

makes a significant and immediate impact

is fast and productive

produces a quantity of work that is consistently high

PRODUCTIVITY

is able to maintain a high level of output without sacrificing quality

is improving productivity without compromising quality

makes effective use of all equipment to sustain a high productive output

provides strong and productive results

produces substantial results

is reliable in producing solid results

generates superior results

produces measurable results

produces at a high and sustainable level

is an abundant producer

exceeds normal output standards

surpasses production goals

outperforms on a consistent basis

delivers consistent high performance

performs at a level that regularly exceeds job requirements

is able to consistently exceed performance expectations

produces beyond normal expectations

produces more than expected

PROFESSIONALISM

demonstrates an exceptional mastery of professional skills

reveals extensive academic preparation

possesses highly acclaimed professional skills

is at the pinnacle of professional excellence

is widely recognized for professional expertise

demonstrates professional expertise

displays well-oriented professional knowledge

communicates on a high professional level

is a seasoned professional

seeks a higher degree of professional excellence

is eager to build professional credentials

welcomes professional challenges

shows concern about professional improvement

sustains a professional growth strategy

enhances professional growth at every opportunity

strives to grow professionally through continuous study and participation

follows professional trends closely

seeks to continuously broaden professional horizons

PROFESSIONALISM

knows when to bring in outside expertise

maintains a high degree of professional participation

develops the skills needed to maintain the highest standards of professional excellence

displays a quality of work that reflects high professional standards

displays high standards of professional behavior

creates a high level of professional trust

demonstrates high standards of professional conduct

promotes a highly professional culture

possesses high professional values

maintains high professional ethics

follows high ethical practices

follows ethical procedures

displays a high level of personal integrity

provides subordinates with definite, positive assistance to correct professional difficulties

develops enduring professional relationships

stimulates professionalism

conveys professionalism

displays loyalty to the profession

(continued)

PROFESSIONALISM

displays a positive attitude to the profession

engenders respect for profession

is highly respected for professional expertise

displays a professional style

displays professional pride

makes excellent impressions

projects a positive image

projects poise and authority

conforms to proper standards of professional dress

dresses appropriately for the position consistent with job requirements

wears appropriate clothing and accessories consistent with job requirements

dresses consistent with organizational expectations

dresses to convey an appropriate image in accordance with position requirements

prepares writings that reflect a polished professional image

writes memos, letters and reports that reflect professional expertise

PROJECT MANAGEMENT

plans, organizes and completes projects in the shortest, most efficient manner

prepares solid project proposals

excels in obtaining management support for projects

is able to obtain the authority needed to successfully complete projects

is skilled in gaining organizational support for projects

is able to obtain needed financial approval in support of projects

is successful in obtaining additional funding when costs exceed original approvals

establishes clear project goals and objectives

demonstrates a systematic approach in carrying out projects

handles projects in logical sequence

makes effective use of all available resources when given a project

seeks project input from multiple sources

excels in building a powerful project management team

encourages the maximum contribution of each team member

keeps in control of projects

(continued)

PROJECT MANAGEMENT

sets realistic timetables to keep projects on target

keeps projects on target and on time

keeps projects on schedule and within budget

is able to keep programs running smoothly

effectively tracks the progress of various projects

excels in vitalizing stalled projects

is able to successfully handle multiple projects at the same time

accepts special projects with enthusiasm

is eager to accept challenging projects

is exceptionally reliable when given a project

displays a strong personal commitment to successfully completing all projects

completes the most complex projects with impressive results

keeps management fully informed of a project's progress

writes reports that contain solid findings and recommendations

makes excellent presentations of completed projects

promotes quality values throughout the organization

places the highest priority on the organization's quality reputation

is successful in obtaining top management support for quality improvement programs

recognizes the importance of quality in providing a competitive edge

is extremely quality conscious

emphasizes quality enhancement

provides total quality assurance

is fully committed to quality assurance

demonstrates an unwavering commitment to quality

strives for state-of-the-art perfection

performs with unusual accuracy, thoroughness and effectiveness

emphasizes quality control and defect prevention at every opportunity

excels in preventing defects

encourages all employees to be alert for defects

effectively uses empowerment to achieve improved quality

(continued)

QUALITY

implements prompt measures to avoid a recurrence of errors

strives for flawless quality

excels in detecting flaws and imperfections

makes effective use of employee communications to build quality awareness

promotes quality awareness

encourages employee suggestions for quality improvements

shows professional concern for quality work

demonstrates accuracy, thoroughness and orderliness in achieving quality

displays pride in work

produces a quality of work that is consistently high

achieves the highest standards of quality excellence

is committed to excellence

makes certain that all incoming materials meet quality standards

ensures that all inspectors are thoroughly trained

establishes high quality goals

recognizes the importance of quality service

RECORDS MANAGEMENT - CONFIDENTIAL RECORDS

keeps affected employees informed of all records that are considered confidential

oversees and effectively maintains the confidentially of vital records

respects and properly maintains confidential records

recognizes the need to protect confidential records

provides strict protection of confidential records

ensures that sensitive records are kept confidential

follows a strict policy of properly identifying all confidential correspondence and records

identifies all mailing envelopes that contain confidential information

seeks approval before copying any confidential information

ensures that affected employees are aware of the need to safeguard confidential information and strictly comply to privacy legislation

follows all privacy policies and procedures outlined in position description

ensures that all employees understand and conform to privacy legislation

possesses a solid knowledge of privacy record keeping laws

(continued)

RECORDS MANAGEMENT - CONFIDENTIAL RECORDS

makes certain that confidential record keeping conforms to all legal requirements

maintains physical, electronic and procedural safeguards to protect personal employee information

keeps confidential records in a secure location

monitors access to all areas containing highly confidential records

respects the need to discuss confidential records in private areas

keeps bystanders from over hearing discussions on private records

safeguards all information that is critical to the organization's future

seeks approval before releasing questionable information

releases records on a need to know basis

is careful to avoid releasing records that would be valuable to competitors

ensures that confidential records are fully secured on all computers

ensures that all computer passwords are closely controlled

follows all privacy policies outlined in job description

ensures that all new employees are informed of the need to protect confidential records

RECORDS MANAGEMENT - OPERATIONAL RECORDS

excels in maintaining an effective record retention program giving proper attention to legal, tax and operating concerns

is very effective in classifying, filing and retrieving documents

is skilled in classifying records for retention, destruction or storage

ensures that all record retention schedules conform to federal, state and local requirements

keeps all departments informed of changes in record retention requirements

keeps well informed of record retention and disclosure requirements

establishes effective systems for records retention

follows a sound records retention schedule

is well aware of the organization's information retrieval requirements

is highly skilled in finding relevant records within a reasonable time

is able to quickly retrieve essential records

is skilled in developing a highly effective information retrieval system

ensures that record keeping procedures are in place and followed by appropriate employees

(continued)

RECORDS MANAGEMENT - OPERATIONAL RECORDS

ensures that all employees follow record keeping procedures

is highly skilled in electronic records management

excels in maintaining electronic files

ensures that electronic records are properly secured and back-up protected

is careful to provide back-up for vital electronic records

excels in converting paper files to digital form

makes certain that departing employees understand computer password procedure

is a very efficient and orderly record keeper

keeps simple records with little duplication

keeps records continuously up-dated

keeps records current

ensures that vital company records are kept in a safe and secure location

maintains vital records under fireproof conditions

excels in indexing records storage cartons

handles information overload with proven skills

is able to cope with the information explosion

complies strictly to all government regulations when recruiting, screening and selecting job applicants

makes effective use of various methods to attract potential employees

uses a variety of recruiting sources

gives consideration to recruiting from within

gives careful attention to employee referrals when recruiting

effectively and objectively reviews resumes

is very skilled in properly conducting job applicant interviews

is able to place applicants at ease during interviews

conveys a positive image to job applicants

is very factual and objective when describing job openings

is very knowledgeable about job requirements

is careful to accurately describe responsibilities and duties for job openings

ensures applicants that employee performance is periodically reviewed

keeps informed of compensation packages for various position levels

informs all applicants of the organization's benefit programs

(continued)

RECRUITING SKILLS

determines carefully and objectively
the qualifications and areas of expertise
among job applicants

seeks factual information when making
judgments about applicant qualifications

is outstanding in screening and assessing job
applicants

ensures that job applicants are informed of
their status within reasonable time periods

is very successful in recruiting employees of
outstanding ability

recruits highly qualified people

is strong in recruiting resourceful and talented
employees

excels in recruiting at the executive level

is exceptional in recruiting applicants who
become long-term employees

recognizes the cost benefits of recruiting
applicants that remain long-term employees

is able to fill jobs within reasonable time

incurs reasonable costs in recruiting

works closely with management and
supervisory personnel when fulfilling
job requirements

is able to thoroughly conduct orientation
programs for new employees

RESILIENCE

is able to recover promptly from disappointments, failures and unfavorable situations

demonstrates a strong ability to recover from setbacks and difficulties

is able to recover and effectively cope with disruptions and disappointments

is very successful in overcoming unfavorable results

displays strong resilience to unfavorable events

is resilient to uncontrollable conditions

strengthens resilience by overcoming difficult situations and unfavorable developments

responds to difficult problems with speed, confidence and strong resilience

remains motivated despite hardships

remains optimistic despite discouraging developments

maintains a positive attitude despite setbacks

is able to maintain a positive outlook regardless of setbacks

maintains enthusiasm despite undesirable outcomes

is able to overcome organizational setbacks with renewed enthusiasm

encourages a positive climate during unfavorable circumstances

RESOURCEFULNESS

demonstrates self-reliance and resourcefulness

is extremely resourceful and enthusiastic

draws on strong personal resources when faced with difficult situations

maximizes individual resources and energies

capitalizes on personal strengths

effectively organizes, assembles and arranges resources to meet goals

effectively matches goals to resources

demonstrates the ability to make maximum use of all resources

makes effective use of all organizational resources

maximizes the use of organizational resources

makes optimum use of organizational resources

optimizes the use of all available resources

maximizes all available resources

demonstrates a tremendous knowledge of resources

excels in drawing on an arsenal of resources to achieve objectives

is able to draw on a variety of resources to achieve results

RESOURCEFULNESS

effectively uses all information sources

is very effective in using the Internet as a powerful resource

makes effective use of information and resources available from industry associations

is able to capitalize on hidden resources

knows when to consult expert resources

develops resourceful solutions

develops resources for future needs

allocates resources wisely

effectively assesses employee resources, strengths and competencies

effectively matches resources with objectives

makes certain that employees have the equipment, tools and resources to achieve results

achieves success when confronted with limited resources

makes reasonable requests for additional resources and assistance

is skilled in obtaining additional resources when necessary

excels in the strategic repositioning of resources

RESPONSIBILITY

devotes appropriate attention to all responsibilities

performs a critical and responsible role

develops job descriptions with clearly defined responsibilities and authorities

keeps all actions within the responsibilities defined in position description

accepts responsibility for own decisions and those of subordinates

assumes responsibility for mistakes and shortcomings of subordinates

takes total responsibility for actions of subordinates

accepts full responsibility for results

is willing to accept ultimate responsibility

is responsible, trustworthy and answerable

honors all commitments

fulfills all obligations

displays responsible conduct

accepts responsibility for compliance with rules and regulations

continues to seek and accept responsibility

seizes responsibility

thrives on greater responsibility

RESPONSIBILITY

is always eager to broaden job responsibilities

takes positive action to meet growing responsibility

delegates responsibility effectively

assigns responsibility effectively

delegates responsibility along with sufficient authority

builds personal accountability

displays a willingness to face conflicts

is willing to confront tough issues

accepts new job assignments willingly

is eager to seek formidable challenges

is eager to accept challenging projects

welcomes challenging assignments

views new responsibilities as an opportunity for growth

welcomes significant challenges

maintains strict oversight responsibility

promotes a high degree of corporate responsibility

establishes policies reflecting strong support of corporate responsibility

RISK-TAKING

ensures that risk-taking is in the best interests of the entire organization

avoids placing the organization at great risk

recognizes the potential benefits of risk-taking

is highly competent in risk assessment and management

effectively manages risks

excels in risk-taking management and analysis

keeps management informed of potential risks

is skilled in identifying potential risks

is very competent in risk and disaster planning

practices sound risk-taking

demonstrates reasonable risk-taking

is an accomplished risk-taker

is a sound risk-taker

turns risk-taking into opportunities

is willing to take risks for long-term rewards

is willing to take risks that achieve exceptional results

is willing to take risks in search of outstanding success

takes short-time risks for long-term gains

RISK-TAKING

does not fear taking risks

is not afraid to take risks

is eager to take risks

takes risks based on sound convictions

follows prudent risk-taking

is willing to take calculated risks

considers all relevant information before engaging in risk-taking

takes risks with reasonable probability of success

is able to make sound estimates of risk-taking probabilities

avoids underestimating potential risks

considers all ramifications before taking risks

considers all potential consequence of risk-taking

explores all possible outcomes before taking risks

considers all potential risks before taking action

evaluates alternative risks

protects against all risks

copes effectively with risks and uncertainly

SAFETY AND SECURITY

promotes safety as a core value of the organization

is able to obtain top management support for strong safety programs

makes safety a number one priority

places a high priority on workplace safety

gives a high priority to safety issues

is highly committed to workplace safety

is very safety conscious

shows concern for worker safety

keeps well informed of safety requirements

maintains meticulous safety records

makes certain that all safety regulations are adhered to

complies with all safety recommendations and requirements

excels in accident prevention management

encourages all employees to make suggestions for safety improvements

makes effective use of safety awards and incentives

is a strong supporter and participant in safety training programs

SAFETY AND SECURITY

seeks to continuously improve the safety of injury-prone job duties

keeps alert to all job hazards

takes prompt action to eliminate work hazards

takes prompt action to eliminate unsafe conditions

is fully aware of all security policies and programs

monitors all security measures on a continuous basis

provides strong computer security measures

excels in providing electronic security measures

uses sophisticated technology to provide security

keeps abreast of new technical devices to provide added security

follows all security measures

adheres to all security policies

enforces rigid procedures to control access to certain areas

reports suspicious activities promptly to security personnel

keeps alert for security break-downs and takes prompt corrective actions

SALES MANAGEMENT

is able to generate consistent sales growth

is very successful in building incremental sales

establishes realistic and attainable sales goals

excels in developing sales objectives that are realistic and effective

meets sales objectives consistently by (_____) percent

keeps alert to new marketing opportunities

responds quickly to changing market conditions

is able to react quickly to changing market trends

shows sustained success in developing new markets

explores new markets on a continuous basis

is continuously searching for high growth markets

excels in developing new markets

excels in expanding geographic markets

ensures that proper attention is devoted to all levels of distribution

gives appropriate attention to all distribution channels

SALES MANAGEMENT

is very successful in developing sales through major marketers

excels in developing major account loyalty

gives appropriate attention to large accounts

is skilled in obtaining high level customer appointments

demonstrates a strong ability to prevent large customers from switching to competitors

takes prompt measures to combat significant competition

is very successful in developing sales through distributors

excels in developing distributor loyalty

gives sufficient attention to smaller accounts to increase sales potential

keeps alert to all sales opportunities

keeps alert to new products

keeps abreast of the latest trends in Internet selling

makes a strong contribution to pricing policies and strategies

is very effective in formulating pricing strategies

keeps pricing strategies consistent with profitability goals

(continued)

SALES MANAGEMENT

keeps aware of customer price perceptions

hires individuals with a high probability
of selling success

excels in retaining talented sales personnel

is able to retain high performance
representatives

excels in developing effective recognition
programs for outstanding sales personnel

is very fair and objective in promoting
sales personnel

provides strong sales incentives

excels in developing a sales organization
that is responsive to customer needs

is very effective in creating a sound
sales organization at every level

recognizes the value of sales training

makes effective use of sales meetings
to motivate and train

is able to make powerful and enthusiastic
presentations at conferences and meetings

is a strong motivator of sales personnel

is continuously monitoring sales progress

ensures that the sales force meets all
commitments

is highly respected by field sales personnel

SALES MANAGEMENT

makes certain that the sales force is properly equipped to maximize sales

ensures that sales personnel are making effective use of all advertising, merchandising programs and selling aids

is very effective in maintaining excellent communications with sales personnel

concentrates on increasing sales rather than administrative functions

is very effective in keeping upper management informed of sales situations

makes effective use of marketing research

monitors changing customer preferences on a continuous basis

monitors on-going packaging preferences

prepares sound sales budgets

monitors sales costs and expenses continuously

keeps well informed of customer payment problems

excels in managing geographically dispersed sales operations

keeps in close contact with regional and district offices

impresses on the entire sales organization the need to treat customers courteously and fairly

SELLING SKILLS

achieves continuous sales growth

is a top sales producer

is a top sales performer

is a solid sales producer

is able to consistently meet sales quotas

is a sales leader

develops sound call frequency patterns

follows effective call frequency patterns

submits excellent call reports

maintains an excellent sales to call ratio

excels in growing a broader customer base

is very creative in generating leads

follows-up on all leads

is very effective in turning leads into sales

turns prospects into well satisfied customers

excels in obtaining new customers

is comfortable in making cold calls

displays strong selling skills

demonstrates persuasive selling skills

is skilled in arousing customer interest

SELLING SKILLS

uses effective sales approaches

displays a strong knowledge of product lines

capitalizes on all product features

excels in selling benefits

places emphasis on customer benefits

focuses on benefits

is able to make effective use of sales training techniques

is highly regarded for recommending new merchandising and selling aids

makes effective use of selling aids

keeps aids current and presentable

makes effective use of advertising and sales promotions

is very effective in creating customer sales promotions

makes outstanding product presentations at customer sales events

gains the full promotional support of marketers

is making effective use of technology to improve sales performance

makes effective use of testimonials

is very skilled in overcoming objections

excels in sales closing

(continued)

SELLING SKILLS

follows sound pricing strategies

sells on the basis of value rather than price

is proficient in overcoming price resistance

is able to successfully overcome sales resistance

recognizes the hidden motivations of customers

excels in uncovering real buying motives

maintains effective control of sales situations

maintains a high degree of selling ethics

makes well prepared sales presentations

uses service as a powerful selling aid

emphasizes service to overcome price objections

sells the value of service

builds on competitive advantages

capitalizes on competitive advantages

is quick to recognize competitive advantages

handles competitive situations with confidence and tact

keeps well informed of the strengths and weaknesses of competitors

makes effective use of competitive analysis

SELLING SKILLS

makes effective use of company strengths to counter competitive offers

keeps sales management informed of trends and developments

offers sound suggestions for improving sales

is very cooperative in sharing information with other sales personnel

is a strong contributor in team selling

is a strong participant in team selling

connects well with customers

strives to continuously improve customer satisfaction

is strong in developing customer satisfaction

concentrates on increasing customer satisfaction

keeps customers satisfied

gains the trust of customers

is highly regarded and trusted by accounts

excels in establishing customer credibility

builds strong credibility with customer personnel

strives to enhance customer loyalty

builds customer loyalty

(continued)

SELLING SKILLS

places a high priority on retaining customers

excels in customer retention

excels in developing repeat customers

maintains continuous customer contact

keeps customers first

builds mutually profitable relationships with customers

builds strong customer relationships

excels in building lasting relationships with customers

excels in building long-term relationships with accounts

excels in reactivating inactive accounts

meets continuous customer requirements

meets continuous customer expectations

displays a strong knowledge of customer's business

provides excellent support in helping customers maintain optimum inventories

is customer-focused

anticipates customer needs

focuses on customer needs

places a high priority in developing effective solutions to customer needs

SELLING SKILLS

understands customer needs and wants

responds quickly to customer needs

is highly responsive to customer needs and demands

responds quickly to customer needs

is responsive to changing customer demands

displays a high level of empathy in customer relations

excels in training new company personnel

gains the full promotional support of marketers

is highly successful in helping marketers develop local advertising and promotional programs

is very effective in training customer sales personnel

effectively enforces company policies without alienating customers

exercises reasonable expense control

takes prompt action on customer complaints

handles customer problems promptly

is highly responsive to customer problems

responds quickly to customer feedback

STRESS

takes measures to prevent stressful situations

plans to deal effectively with anticipated stressful situations

makes strong mental preparations for stressful situations

is very successful in encouraging acceptance of new methods, procedures and other changes

is able to effectively manage change and promote acceptance

develops programs for coping with the repercussions of changes

copes effectively with the repercussions of changes

is able to capably adjust to ever changing work environments

provides support to employees coping with change

adjusts promptly and calmly to change

implements positive measures to relieve employee anxiety

handles stress and anxiety effectively

copes effectively with anxiety

is able to cope with pressure and maintain composure

copes effectively with pressures and tension

performs well under pressure

remains courteous under pressure

remains calm under pressure

shows poise when under pressure

works effectively in high pressure situations

gains control over job pressures

copes effectively with adversity

is able to cope with adverse conditions

handles emergencies with coolness

is able to stay focused when faced with emergency situations

stays focused under turbulent conditions

maintains coolness despite annoyances

shows a strong resistance to annoyances

copes effectively with uncomfortable situations

works effectively for multiple superiors

copes successfully with demands from superiors, subordinates and peers

effectively handles multiple demands from superiors and subordinates

is able to balance competing priorities

meets ever changing demands

(continued)

STRESS

effectively copes with the stress of demanding duties

keeps stress from affecting job performance

does not allow stress to affect sound decision making

copes effectively with staff reductions

remains calm and professional when faced with tight deadlines

copes effectively with deadlines

performs effectively despite sudden deadlines and changing priorities

keeps situations in perspective

schedules work effectively to avoid stressful situations

plans effectively for crisis situations

excels in crisis prevention

is well prepared to manage a variety of crises

takes quick action during a crisis

remains calm in crisis situations

performs well in crisis situations

handles crises with composure

is not controlled by events and crisis situations

remains calm in emotionally charged situations

remains powerful and effective while under stress

handles authority capably when confronted

keeps calm and professional under the toughest situations

works calmly in a turbulent environment

handles unusual dilemmas with calmness

is calm, cool and collected

displays a calm demeanor

gets things done calmly

displays impressive poise under stress

maintains poise in the toughest situations

maintains composure in high stress situations

maintains composure during stressful circumstances

copes effectively with risk and uncertainly

handles the unexpected with coolness

copes effectively with unintended consequences

recognizes stress-related problems

is able to build a strong resistance to stress

(continued)

STRESS

effectively manages stress

keeps stress under control

maintains control in all situations

maintains strong control in highly charged situations

remains in solid control while under stress

demonstrates coolness under stress

shows finesse in situations of stress

thrives on stressful situations

handles potentially volatile situations with coolness

makes positive use of stress to improve performance

makes effective use of humor to ease tensions

shows compassion for employees who are undergoing difficult situations

takes measures to prevent long-term stress

recognizes the impact of stress and burn out on organizational effectiveness

knows when to seek help

SUPERVISORY SKILLS

excels in the supervision and leadership of subordinates

is a highly respected supervisor

excels in getting work done by others

makes certain that employees have a clear understanding of their responsibilities

develops precise job expectations

establishes realistic work demands

ensures cost-efficient assignment of employees

divides work into manageable activities

effectively schedules personnel for peak and slack periods

effectively balances work flow

effectively prevents over-staffing

gains maximum productivity from employees

optimizes productivity

makes maximum use of personnel and equipment

excels in equipment utilization

maximizes the performance of people and equipment

excels in preventing machinery breakdowns

(continued)

SUPERVISORY SKILLS

maintains consistency of operations

takes prompt action to minimize down time

quickly eliminates trouble spots

strives to make more meaningful and challenging contributions to the betterment of the department

effectively motivates subordinates to exert the effort necessary to attain organizational goals

maintains a work situation which stimulates the growth of individuals

uses job enrichment to improve productivity

expects and demands superior performance

places emphasis on results

brings out the best in employees

gives constant encouragement to subordinates

gives constructive suggestions to subordinates

takes effective measures to eliminate job plateauing

keeps employees challenged through job enrichment

challenges the abilities of subordinates

recognizes the important relationships between rewards, reinforcement and results

SUPERVISORY SKILLS

motivates and rewards employees for exceptional performance

maximizes the value of recognition and rewards

gives proper recognition

makes effective use of constructive compliments

excels in giving verbal praise

develops a climate providing motivation, participation and opportunities for employee initiative

promotes an effective climate

encourages a climate for action

develops a productive work environment

promotes a performance-oriented environment

promotes a comfortable, friendly organizational atmosphere

is readily accessible to subordinates

excels in encouraging employee involvement

encourages active involvement of staff

receives full support from staff

promotes positive involvement

stimulates individual participation

(continued)

SUPERVISORY SKILLS

stimulates productive discussion sessions for positive action

effectively seeks and obtains ideas

asserts ideas effectively

asserts authority effectively

effectively communicates organizational policies and other information to subordinates

is effective in giving orders and directions

gives clear instructions

avoids over-supervising

effectively utilizes experienced employees to train new hires

effectively supervises employees with more experience

effectively supervises former peers

effectively supervises temporary employees

makes effective use of temporary employees to meet immediate needs

plans effectively for seasonal fluctuations in work force requirements

gives sound, practical advice

gains employee confidence

shows concern for the employee as a person

SUPERVISORY SKILLS

develops strong credibility with subordinates

understands different personalities and traits

manages diverse personalities with skill

shows empathy

is sensitive to the feelings of others

respects and values employees

shows genuine respect

shows warmth and consideration

treats employees with dignity and respect

supervises firmly and fairly

is fair and firm when dealing with subordinates

establishes acceptable tolerance levels

effectively handles employee problems and discontent

handles employee problems professionally

recognizes and deals with signs of employee unrest

encourages constructive feedback

responds quickly to feedback

turns complaints into opportunities

knows when to reprimand

(continued)

SUPERVISORY SKILLS

knows when to ignore

knows when to confront

maintains order and discipline

effectively handles negative behavior

handles disruptive behavior with firmness

disciplines inappropriate behavior promptly

disciplines without compromising authority

disciplines without causing resentment

uses positive techniques to discipline

uses constructive discipline

settles disciplinary problems quickly

handles behavior problems promptly
before they become irreversible

takes prompt measures to prevent
performance and behavior problems

keeps small situations from becoming big
problems

takes prompt corrective action

handles problems immediately

corrects without criticizing

takes appropriate remedial action

SUPERVISORY SKILLS

dispels unfounded rumors quickly

settles disputes firmly

resolves conflicts constructively

is skilled in conflict resolution

monitors absenteeism and tardiness closely

gives appropriate attention to reducing
absenteeism, tardiness and turnover

effectively controls employee absenteeism and
tardiness

enforces attendance rules strictly and uniformly

handles chronic absenteeism decisively

overcomes personality conflicts

prevents personnel conflicts from reducing
productivity

effectively manages the marginal performer

excels in revitalizing employees who are
coasting

effectively handles difficult people

is skilled in supervising difficult people

effectively handles resistance from staff
members

deals effectively with resistance

(continued)

SUPERVISORY SKILLS

effectively deals with mistakes and errors

takes positive steps to avoid recurrence of errors

copes effectively with misunderstandings

keeps well informed of new legislation affecting the workplace

maintains strict compliance with employment laws

keeps well informed of supervisory legal responsibilities

is able to take disciplinary action while conforming to all legal aspects

applies all rules and regulations fairly

reports all incidents promptly

prepares solid documentation before disciplining problem workers

ensures that all personnel problems are properly documented

documents employee disciplinary action promptly and thoroughly

follows all operating procedures closely

deals effectively with tough workplace challenges

TACT AND DIPLOMACY

is very confident in handling awkward situations

handles situations in a calm, polished manner

handles sensitive situations with confidence

accomplishes results without creating friction

handles complaints with tact

avoids arguments

disagrees without offending

makes tactful and appropriate responses

effectively handles conflicts and confrontations

handles confrontations constructively

is very tactful when facing confrontations

is tactful in conflict situations

is very diplomatic in settling disputes

is very diplomatic in achieving mutual agreement

refuses requests with tact and diplomacy

is very polished in denying requests

is cordial, tactful and firm

displays trust and mutual understanding

employs procedures that reveal poise

(continued)

TACT AND DIPLOMACY

admits mistakes and errors with tact

is tactful in correcting the mistakes of others

offers constructive criticism without creating resentment

accepts constructive criticism

is able to respond to criticism without being defensive

is very polished in matters of etiquette

demonstrates polished etiquette skills

displays proper etiquette

employs procedures that reveal poise

handles visitors with grace and tact

displays grace and style

excels in welcoming new employees

is exceptionally polished in making introductions

follows proper protocol

is very polished when handling delicate situations

is polite in all situations

displays excellent mannerisms

conveys sincere appreciation at every opportunity

develops an organizational culture that fosters teamwork

excels in obtaining the management support and authorities needed for team success

sets clear goals and objectives of the team

establishes realistic schedules for achieving team objective

excels in developing vibrant leadership teams

excels in building teams for success

is a strong team builder

builds strong teams to meet performance goals

builds a spirited team effort

excels in developing self-managed teams

excels in appointing people with complimentary skills for maximum team effort

excels in appointing interdisciplinary team members

makes maximum use of the diverse talents of team members

capitalizes on the talents of all team members

effectively draws on the strengths of all team members

makes effective use of team resources

(continued)

TEAM SKILLS

expects all team members to make maximum contributions

is a strong contributor to a team's success

makes a valuable contribution to team objectives

encourages the full participation of all team members

provides management with periodic reports of the team's progress

uses the synergistic power of team planning to achieve goals

uses the synergistic power of teamwork to achieve results

excels in task-oriented team development

excels in developing harmony and greater productivity

implements self-directed teams successfully

resolves team conflicts with finesse

promotes powerful team dynamics

keeps team members fully energized

excels in developing team momentum, enthusiasm and pride

TECHNICAL SKILLS

recognizes the many benefits of spirited technical teamwork

strives for maximum technical team performance

recognizes the value of technical team dynamics

builds a strong sense of technical teamwork and purpose

develops strong camaraderie among technical team members

excels in technology management

effectively blends management skills with technical expertise

is well recognized for technological expertise

demonstrates strong technical expertise

demonstrates sound scientific and technical expertise

demonstrates a high level of technical competence

possesses highly specialized technical skills

demonstrates strong technical knowledge

follows emerging science, technology issues and trends

keeps abreast of emerging technologies

(continued)

TECHNICAL SKILLS

keeps well informed of advanced technologies

makes effective use of technological advances

places a high priority on modernization and enhanced technology

is strategically upgrading technology

keeps informed of new technologies in office automation

displays a thorough understanding of computer technology

incorporates the newest computer technologies

excels in using information technology to reduce costs

uses the latest techniques to gain the competitive edge

overcomes resistance to technological change

is skilled in overcoming technical barriers

understands sophisticated technical specifications

is able to write technical information in easily understood terms

makes effective use of graphics to present highly technical information

makes effective use of technical support

strives for significant technological breakthroughs

TIME MANAGEMENT

achieves maximum time effectiveness

places a high value on time effectiveness

demonstrates effective allocation of time resources

deals effectively with distractions

identifies and eliminates time wasters

avoids time snares

uses systematic methods to accomplish more in less time

makes effective use of computer technology to increase available time

works smarter, not harder

saves time by concentrating on value added activities

avoids becoming involved in endless details

delegates for maximum time effectiveness

sets realistic time goals

is reliable in achieving results within expected time periods

meets all deadlines consistently

makes effective use of peak time periods

maximizes peak times

uses time wisely

VENDOR RELATIONS

selects vendors on the basis of comparative and objective analysis

weighs technical and research capabilities when selecting sources of supply

ensures that vendors are able to provide strong technical and service support

is skilled in using multiple sources to provide leverage on material costs

excels in using multiple sources for ensuring competitive costs and uninterrupted supply

builds a high level of trust with key suppliers

is able to maintain a friendly but professional relationship with vendors

enforces vendor compliance to the company's procurement policies

ensures that vendors conform to strict contractual requirements regarding the confidentially of trade secrets, formulas, processes, manufacturing equipment etc.

makes certain that all supplier contracts are in compliance with government regulations

keeps vendors informed of the need for compliance to ethical policies

displays high personal integrity when dealing with suppliers

is firm but fair in relationships with vendors

VENDOR RELATIONS

is a strong negotiator with vendors

maintains accurate and up-dated profiles
of all vendors

expects vendors to provide advance notice
of possible problems involving strikes,
raw material shortages, natural disasters
and other situations affecting product
availability

is very reliable in keeping management
informed of significant developments
with major suppliers

is highly skilled in providing a continuous
flow of materials to ensure uninterrupted
production

excels in preventing production shut-downs
due to component shortages

works closely with vendors to keep abreast
of industry developments and trends

keeps vendors informed of changing market
demands involving seasons, styles, colors,
sizes etc.

facilitates vendor contacts with research,
manufacturing and marketing personnel

is very effective in utilizing the resources
of key departments in support of vendor
relations

makes effective use of supplier expertise

displays a strong ability to utilize the
specialized knowledge of vendors

(continued)

VENDOR RELATIONS

makes certain that key supplier personnel and back-up assistants are always available for immediate contact

is continuously evaluating vendor performance

makes periodic visits to supplier facilities for evaluation purposes

gives a high priority to vendors who consistently meet specifications

ensures that all vendors meet tolerances and specification requirements

works closely with quality inspection personnel and promptly alerts vendors of problems

takes prompt corrective action whenever vendor quality problems arise

provides vendors with sufficient lead time

is reliable in keeping suppliers well informed of all manufacturing and warehouse shut-downs

is very successful in obtaining expedited shipments to meet critical situations

works closely with suppliers to ensure just-in-time deliveries

excels in handling complaints, product rejections and recalls with vendors

expresses appreciation for outstanding vendor support

VERSATILITY

Is very capable of handling a multitude of situations

possess an unique combination of skills

demonstrates diversified skills

displays versatile expertise

possesses many talents and capabilities

is extremely versatile

demonstrates competence in many areas

demonstrates excellence in many varied functions

is able to apply skills in a wide variety of areas

demonstrates excellence in performing many different functions

draws on broad experience to capably perform many valued functions

is able to handle multiple projects at the same time

works effectively for multiple supervisors in many varied areas

is highly skilled in multi-tasking

effectively handles concurrent assignments

(continued)

VERSATILITY

performs a broad range of assignments
with efficiency and accuracy

is receptive to changing job responsibilities

is a catalyst for changing responsibilities

deals effectively with a variety of changing
issues

responds quickly to changing job demands

effectively copes with varied and
accelerating job changes

is flexible and open toward changing job
functions

embraces changing duties

is highly adaptive to changes

displays flexibility in adapting to
changing conditions

is able to provide broad organizational support
in many areas

provides strong back-up support during
vacations periods and absences

is extremely valuable in providing back-up
support for other jobs

is successfully showing the ability to develop
from a specialist to a generalist

is a visionary planner

is a visionary thinker

excels in visionary thinking

takes a visionary approach to problems and opportunities

displays a visionary spirit

displays positive vision

displays multi-faceted vision

displays long-term vision

develops strategic vision

excels in visionary strategies

is skilled in accurately visualizing outcomes

demonstrates keen foresight

is able to turn visions into actual action

is able to turn visions into reality

demonstrates an ability to transfer vision into realities

inspires visions of future success

promotes a strong vision of the organization's future

WRITING SKILLS

writes letters, memos and reports that command attention and achieve results

is an accomplished writer

effectively and efficiently handles correspondence

ensures that correspondence is reader-friendly

is skilled in writing letters and messages that cover a wide range of employee happenings

is skilled in writing letters for all occasions

makes effective use of electronic writing

writes clearly, tactfully and effectively

writes tactfully on unpopular subjects

is highly skilled in writing on controversial subjects

excels in creative writing

demonstrates creative writing ability

writes with original thoughts and ideas

writes with remarkable clarity and consistency

writes precisely and effectively

writes with extreme accuracy

uses well documented facts when writing

writes with enthusiasm

writes to convey a positive impression

writes in a positive tone

writes in a positive manner to reflect favorably upon the organization

writes to ensure readability

keeps writing short and simple

places emphasis on meaningful action words

writes lively sentences that gain attention

demonstrates strong grammar and usage skills

displays strong skills in using correct grammar and punctuation

possesses a large vocabulary

is able to clearly express views in writing

is often sought for writing ability

is always willing to provide writing assistance

writes reports that achieve maximum impact

prepares concise and meaningful reports

meets writing deadlines consistently

prepares timely and excellent reports

is a strong contributor in writing annual reports

(continued)

WRITING SKILLS

is highly skilled in preparing reports and proposals

writes proposals that win approval

writes with persuasion

writes powerful presentations

is skilled in writing accurate and well documented performance appraisals

is a skilled speech writer

writes speeches that convey a strong impact

is skilled in writing speeches that capture audiences

excels in converting complex information into simple, readable form

is skilled in using technical terminology

is very proficient in writing manuals, policies and procedures

excels in preparing professional manuals

is very skilled in writing clear instructions

is a highly competent proofreader

demonstrates strong proofreading skills

demonstrates strong editing skills

excels in rewriting, editing and proofreading

II. TWO WORD PHRASES

accelerating changes

accepting responsibility

accomplishing results

accumulated knowledge

accurate assessments

accurate documentation

accurate evaluations

accurate predictions

achievement-driven

achievement-oriented

achieving excellence

achieving results

action plans

active participant

administrative advancements

administrative competence

administrative effectiveness

administrative support

advanced technologies

alternative solutions

analytical approach

(continued)

TWO WORD PHRASES

analytical methods

analytical qualities

analytical reasoning

analytical techniques

analytical thinking

anticipated performance

appropriate attention

appropriate measures

articulate communicator

available resources

basic strengths

broad-minded

broad perspective

broadest discretion

budget discipline

calculated risks

career building

career development

challenge-oriented

challenging opportunities

challenging problems

TWO WORD PHRASES

changing assignments

changing conditions

changing priorities

changing situations

clear expectations

close cooperation

cognitive ability

committed enthusiasm

communication skills

competent communicator

competent performer

competing priorities

competitive advantage

competitive drive

competitive edge

complex information

computer application

computer generated

computer technologies

concentrated effort

conceptual ideas

213

(continued)

TWO WORD PHRASES

concurrent assignments

confident speaker

confident performer

conflict resolution

considerable flexibility

consistent achiever

consistent growth

consistent performance

consistent progress

consistently high

consistently punctual

constructive actions

constructive criticism

constructive discipline

constructive feedback

constructive ideas

contingency plans

continued success

continuing confidence

continuing efforts

continuous improvement

TWO WORD PHRASES

control measures

controlling expenses

conventional wisdom

conveying professionalism

cooperative spirit

core capabilities

core competencies

core components

core principles

core problems

core responsibility

core strengths

core values

corporate culture

corrective actions

corrective measures

cost conscious

cost considerations

cost control

cost effectiveness

cost implications

215

(continued)

TWO WORD PHRASES

cost priorities

cost reductions

creating value

creative alternatives

creative excellence

creative improvements

creative solutions

creative strategies

creative strengths

creative support

creative talent

creative techniques

creative thinking

crisis management

crisis prevention

crisis situations

critical achievement

critical challenges

critical elements

critical factors

critical importance

TWO WORD PHRASES

critical incidents

critical insights

critical role

critical skills

critical solutions

critical thinker

crucial planning

cumulative effects

customer conscious

customer focused

customer-oriented

customer satisfaction

damage control

decisive action

dedicated commitment

dedicated focus

demanding situations

desired results

determined efforts

developing solutions

disciplinary action

(continued)

217

TWO WORD PHRASES

disciplined approach

distinguishing characteristics

diverse talents

diversified approaches

diversified skills

documented facts

driving force

dynamic impressions

dynamic performance

effective presentations

effective systems

efficient manner

electronic capabilities

emerging technologies

emerging trends

eminently qualified

empowerment skills

energetic leader

energy drive

enhanced performance

enterprising performance

TWO WORD PHRASES

enthusiastic commitment

enthusiastic momentum

enthusiastic spirit

environmental leadership

essential activities

essential knowledge

essential skill

ethical conduct

exceeds expectations

exceptional improvement

exceptional outcomes

exceptional progress

expected production

expert consultation

extra efforts

extremely industrious

extremely reliable

extremely resourceful

fast-paced

favorable image

favorable impact

(continued)

TWO WORD PHRASES

favorable impression

financial discipline

first impressions

focused efforts

foremost accountability

formidable challenges

formidable development

forward-looking

forward-thinking

fresh enthusiasm

fresh ideas

fresh insights

fresh perspective

fresh thinking

full participation

fullest participation

fullest support

fully documented

fully prepared

future challenges

future-oriented

TWO WORD PHRASES

global perspective

goal achiever

goal attainment

goal seeker

greater achievement

greater challenge

greater contribution

greater visibility

greatest return

growth potential

growth trajectory

hands-on

heuristic thinking

hidden potential

hidden strengths

hidden talents

high achiever

high enthusiasm

high impact

high momentum

high output

(continued)

TWO WORD PHRASES

high payoff

high potential

high producer

high profile

high quality

high recognition

high spirited

highest priority

highly acclaimed

highly adaptive

highly articulate

highly capable

highly committed

highly competent

highly creditable

highly dependable

highly effective

highly energized

highly focused

highly proficient

highly promotable

TWO WORD PHRASES

highly regarded

highly respected

highly sophisticated

highly supportive

highly talented

highly valuable

ideally positioned

imaginative innovation

imaginative solutions

imaginative thinking

impeccable honesty

implementing change

important contributor

important role

impressive results

impressive zeal

improving quality

improving techniques

increasing efficiency

incremental improvements

independent decisions

(continued)

TWO WORD PHRASES

individual strengths

individual values

information sources

initiating solutions

inner drive

innovative developments

innovative insight

innovative planning

innovative possibilities

innovative solutions

innovative thinking

innovative trends

intellectual horizons

intense desire

intuitive ability

intuitive judgments

job enlargement

job enrichment

job plateauing

keen interest

key challenges

TWO WORD PHRASES

key characteristics

key element

key employee

key role

key values

key variables

leadership qualities

leadership role

leading edge

learning curve

learning experience

learning opportunities

logical sequence

logical thinking

loyal support

maintaining control

maintaining focus

maintaining momentum

major contributor

management effectiveness

management efficiency

(continued)

TWO WORD PHRASES

management expectations

management principles

management support

marked enthusiasm

maximizing resources

maximum contribution

maximum effectiveness

maximum efficiency

maximum effort

maximum impact

maximum productivity

maximum results

maximum return

maximum success

measurable results

meets expectations

mental toughness

meticulous attention

minimum supervision

most respected

multi-faceted

TWO WORD PHRASES

multi-tasking

multiple demands

multiple resources

multiple skills

multiple superiors

mutual success

new approaches

new concepts

new perspectives

new strategies

new technologies

newly created

notable achievement

open communications

open-minded

operating knowledge

operating skills

operational excellence

opinion leader

optimal effectiveness

optimal levels

(continued)

TWO WORD PHRASES

optimal outcomes

optimal results

optimal targets

optimistic attitude

optimum advantage

optimum productivity

optional solutions

organizational culture

organizational effectiveness

organizational expectations

organizational goals

organizational resources

organizational support

organizational transition

peak efficiency

peak performance

performance conscious

performance impact

performance levels

performance measurement

performance peak

TWO WORD PHRASES

performance targets

personal accountability

personal charisma

personal commitment

personal effectiveness

personal growth

personal impact

personal integrity

personal magnetism

personal strengths

personal traits

personal values

personal visibility

persuasive ability

pivotal role

planning approaches

planning decisions

planning solutions

planning techniques

positive actions

positive approach

(continued)

TWO WORD PHRASES

positive attitude

positive attributes

positive direction

positive expectations

positive feedback

positive force

positive image

positive impact

positive influence

positive intervention

positive outlook

positive reinforcement

positive tone

powerful commitment

powerful insights

practical advice

practical applications

practical insights

practical skills

practical solutions

practical thinking

TWO WORD PHRASES

premier position

preeminent authority

prime mover

priority determinations

problem prevention

problem solving

productive cooperation

productive impact

professional competence

professional development

professional effectiveness

professional ethics

professional excellence

professional expertise

professional participation

professional skills

professional trends

profit-conscious

profit-minded

profit-oriented

profound impact

(continued)

TWO WORD PHRASES

promoting teamwork

prompt measures

proper perspective

proven capabilities

proven performer

proven record

proven techniques

quality enhancement

quality conscious

quality improvement

rating inflation

realistic approach

realistic objectives

realistic solutions

remarkable record

renewed energy .

resource utilization

resourceful solutions

results-focused

results-oriented

risk-taking

TWO WORD PHRASES

robust impact

root causes

routine tasks

safety conscious

sales opportunities

sales producer

satisfying solutions

secretarial support

self-confident

self-development

self-directed

self-discipline

self-esteem

self-motivated

self-pacing

self-reliant

self-starter

sensitive situations

serious-minded

shared drive

shared knowledge

(continued)

TWO WORD PHRASES

shared values

shared vision

significant accomplishments

significant contribution

significant impact

significant progress

significant results

significant role

simplified solutions

skill development

skilled communicator

skilled writer

smooth transition

solid achiever

solid background

solid contributor

solid control

solid direction

solid documentation

solid experience

solid foundation

TWO WORD PHRASES

solid growth

solid performer

solid reputation

solid skills

solid techniques

solution-driven

solution seeker

sound approach

sound conclusions

sound consideration

sound controls

sound decisions

sound judgment

sound perspectives

special assignments

specialized skills

speech proficiency

stabilizing influence

steady growth

steady progress

stellar record

(continued)

TWO WORD PHRASES

stimulating action

strategic alternatives

strategic opportunities

strategic plans

strategic priorities

strategic repositioning

strategic thrust

strategic vision

strategically focused

strategically-oriented

strategically positioned

strategically sound

stress tolerance

stressful situations

stressful solutions

strong achiever

strong contributor

strong credibility

strong effort

strong growth

strong impact

TWO WORD PHRASES

strong motivator

strong performer

strong perseverance

strong potential

strong producer

strongly committed

strongly qualified

substantial achievement

substantial contribution

success-driven

success-oriented

successful conclusion

superior growth

support services

supportive relationships

supportive skills

sustainable growth

sustainable results

sustained commitment

sustained development

sustained energy

(continued)

TWO WORD PHRASES

sustained performance

sustained success

synergistic benefit

synergistic power

systematic approach

systematic results

task priorities

team building

team dynamics

team effort

team motivator

team performance

team spirit

technical competence

technically advanced

technical competence

thinks futuristically

thinks globally

time conscious

time-efficient

top performer

TWO WORD PHRASES

total involvement

tracking progress

training needs

trend setter

trouble shooting

true potential

ultimate responsibility

unanticipated consequences

unintended consequences

unified efforts

unique capabilities

unique challenges

unique combination

unique expertise

unique insights

unique knowledge

unique methods

unique opportunities

unique perspective

unique resource

unique talents

(continued)

TWO WORD PHRASES

unique value

uniquely positioned

uniquely qualified

unparalleled opportunities

untapped potential

unwavering commitment

valuable asset

valuable resource

value creation

verbal commitments

viable solutions

visionary leadership

visionary spirit

visionary strategies

vital role

well informed

well positioned

well qualified

working knowledge

world-class

zero tolerances

III. HELPFUL ADJECTIVES

absolute

abundant

accurate

active

adaptable

adept

affirmative

alert

ambitious

analytical

articulate

authoritative

calm

capable

challenging

charismatic

clear-thinking

cohesive

compelling

competent

complete

composed

comprehensive

concise

confident

conscientious

considerable

consistent

constructive

cooperative

courageous

courteous

creative

curious

decisive

dedicated

definite

dependable

desirable

determined

diligent

diplomatic

(continued)

HELPFUL ADJECTIVES

discreet	fine
distinctive	flawless
dynamic	flexible
eager	forceful
effective	foremost
efficient	formidable
eminent	forward-looking
energetic	frank
enlightening	genuine
enterprising	good-natured
enthusiastic	graceful
essential	great
excellent	hands-on
exceptional	harmonious
exciting	helpful
extra	high
extraordinary	high-tech
extreme	honest
factual	imaginative
fair	immense
favorable	impeccable

HELPFUL ADJECTIVES

important	major
independent	mature
industrious	maximum
influential	meaningful
informative	meticulous
ingenious	motivated
innovative	neat
instrumental	objective
intense	observant
interactive	obvious
inventive	open-minded
invigorative	opportunistic
involved	optimal
keen	optimistic
knowledgeable	orderly
lasting	organized
latent	original
latest	outstanding
logical	patient
loyal	perceptive
magnificent	perfect

(continued)

HELPFUL ADJECTIVES

persevering	punctual
persistent	quick
persuasive	rational
pleasant	realistic
poised	relentless
positive	reliable
powerful	remarkable
practical	resilient
pragmatic	resourceful
precise	respectful
predictable	responsive
preeminent	rigorous
premier	self-confident
proactive	self-demanding
productive	significant
professional	sincere
profound	sizable
progressive	sophisticated
prolific	sound
prominent	special
proper	splendid

HELPFUL ADJECTIVES

steadfast

stellar

stern

stimulating

stringent

strong

successful

superb

superior

supportive

sustainable

synergistic

systematic

tactful

tedious

thorough

trustworthy

truthful

ultimate

unique

unlimited

unmatched

untiring

unusual

unwavering

utmost

valuable

versatile

viable

vibrant

vigorous

winning

worthy

IV. HELPFUL VERBS

accelerates

accentuates

accepts

accomplishes

accounts

achieves

acquaints

acquires

activates

acts

actuates

adapts

addresses

adheres

adjusts

administers

adopts

advances

advises

aligns

allocates

amplifies

analyzes

anticipates

applies

appoints

appraises

appropriates

approves

arises

arranges

articulates

ascends

ascertains

aspires

assembles

asserts

assesses

assigns

assimilates

assists

assumes

HELPFUL VERBS

assures

attains

attempts

attends

attracts

audits

augments

authorizes

averts

avoids

broadens

builds

calculates

capitalizes

captivates

centralizes

challenges

checks

circulates

clarifies

clears

coaches

collaborates

collects

combines

commands

communicates

compels

compiles

completes

complies

composes

comprehends

computes

conceives

concentrates

concludes

condenses

conducts

conforms

conjects

considers

(continued)

HELPFUL VERBS

consolidates

consults

consummates

contemplates

continues

contributes

controls

converts

conveys

cooperates

coordinates

copes

corrects

creates

cultivates

decentralizes

decreases

dedicates

defines

delegates

delivers

demonstrates

deploys

deserves

designates

designs

determines

develops

devises

directs

discharges

discovers

discusses

displays

disseminates

distinguishes

distributes

documents

drafts

earns

edits

educates

HELPFUL VERBS

elevates

elicits

eliminates

emanates

embellishes

embraces

emphasizes

employs

empowers

emulates

enables

encompasses

encourages

energizes

enforces

engages

engenders

enhances

enlightens

enriches

ensures

enunciates

envisions

establishes

estimates

evaluates

evidences

evokes

examines

exceeds

excels

executes

exemplifies

exercises

exerts

exhibits

expands

expects

expedites

explores

expresses

extends

(continued)

HELPFUL VERBS

extracts

faces

facilitates

focuses

follows-up

forecasts

foresees

forms

formulates

fosters

fulfills

furnishes

gains

generates

gives

grasps

guides

handles

helps

identifies

impacts

implements

impresses

improves

improvises

increases

influences

informs

initiates

inspects

inspires

installs

instigates

instills

institutes

instructs

insures

integrates

interacts

interns

interprets

interviews

HELPFUL VERBS

introduces	monitors
invents	motivates
investigates	necessitates
invests	negotiates
invokes	neutralizes
issues	notifies
judges	observes
keeps	obtains
knows	operates
launches	optimizes
leads	orchestrates
learns	orders
lectures	organizes
maintains	originates
makes	overcomes
markets	oversees
maximizes	paces
mediates	participates
meets	perceives
minimizes	performs
mobilizes	perpetuates

(continued)

HELPFUL VERBS

plans	realizes
possesses	receives
practices	recognizes
predicts	recommends
prepares	reconciles
presents	records
presumes	recruits
prevents	reduces
prioritizes	refines
processes	reflects
procures	regards
produces	reinforces
programs	rejects
projects	relates
promotes	releases
proposes	relies
protects	reports
provides	represents
pursues	requires
radiates	researches
reaches	resolves

HELPFUL VERBS

resonates	stimulates
respects	strengthens
responds	strives
restores	structures
retains	studies
reviews	submits
revises	suggests
revitalizes	supervises
schedules	supports
secures	surmounts
seeks	surpasses
seizes	surveys
sells	sustains
serves	takes
settles	targets
shows	thinks
simplifies	thrives
solves	tolerates
sorts	trains
sparks	transacts
specifies	translates

(continued)

HELPFUL VERBS

treats

uncovers

understands

undertakes

unifies

uses

utilizes

verifies

vitalizes

weighs

widens

works

writes

V. PERFORMANCE RANKINGS

exceptional

extraordinary

excellent

distinguished

outstanding

very good

good

superior

fair

satisfactory

substandard

unsatisfactory

unacceptable

exceeds expectations

meets expectations

fails to meet expectations

VI. TIME SEQUENCE

always

usually

frequently

often

continuously

sometimes

occasionally

rarely

seldom

never

VII. GUIDELINES FOR SUCCESSFUL EVALUATIONS

I. RATE OBJECTIVELY

You can improve the accuracy of your ratings by recognizing the following factors that subvert evaluations:

1. THE HALO EFFECT:

The tendency of an evaluator to rate a person good or bad on all characteristics based on an experience or knowledge involving only one dimension.

2. LENIENCY TENDENCY:

A tendency toward evaluating all persons as outstanding and to give inflated ratings rather than true assessments of performance.

3. STRICTNESS TENDENCY:

The opposite of the leniency tendency; that is, a bias toward rating all persons at the low end of the scale and a tendency to be overly demanding or critical.

4. AVERAGE TENDENCY:

A tendency to evaluate every person as average regardless of major differences in performance.

Legislation, court cases and government directives have added a new dimension to the performance appraisal process.

Employee evaluations may become a key issue in litigation. Clearly, the accuracy of performance appraisals is a requirement of the highest priority.

II. USE SIGNIFICANT DOCUMENTATION AND FACTUAL EXAMPLES

It is essential that performance evaluations be measured in relation to any pre-existing standards, objectives or other specific job requirements.

Most appraisal systems require the rater to cite examples of performance. Examples should be objective and specific rather than subjective and general.

Whenever possible, use quantitative examples which can be expressed in numerical terms using figures, percentages or amounts. For example, it is preferable to state "exceeded sales objective by 10% through the first six months" rather than "exceeded sales objective."

III. PLAN FOR APPRAISAL INTERVIEW

The appraisal interview is one of the most important elements of the evaluation process. The purpose of the interview is to review performance and let people know how they are doing. You can improve the effectiveness of the interview by adhering to the following guidelines:

select a quiet, comfortable and appropriate location

plan to avoid interruptions

allow ample time for the discussion

(continued)

sit aside of the person

put the person at ease

conduct the interview in a positive manner

review the ratings by category

keep the interview performance-oriented

encourage the person to talk, but remain firmly in control

listen carefully

avoid the defensive

focus on patterns rather than isolated instances

respond to objections, problems and disagreements

concentrate on facts

be honest

be a coach, not a judge

place emphasis on positive reinforcement

develop positive action plans

end the interview on a positive and supportive basis

IV. EMPHASIZE FUTURE DEVELOPMENT

Effective performance appraisal programs place emphasis on planning for future development. The attainment of organizational goals coupled with maximum employee growth is the mark of true management success. You can develop the full potential of subordinates by implementing the following:

1. Analyze performance and develop appropriate strategies for strengthening areas in need of improvement.

2. Develop a goal-oriented plan to prepare for greater responsibility.

3. Establish follow-up plans to ensure employee growth.

4. Use positive reinforcement to motivate.

V. EMPHASIZE THE POSITIVE

The positive use of performance appraisals combined with sound management practice will contribute to the improved effectiveness of every organization.

VIII. INDEX

WORDS APPEARING UNDER MULTIPLE CONTENT HEADINGS

INDEX

(continued)

INDEX

(continued)

INDEX

ISBN 978-1-882423-20-0

51595
9 781882 423200